15

W. W. Denslow

The Other Wizard of Oz

Joseph Christian Leyendecker (1874-1951)
Portrait of W. W. Denslow, ca. 1898.
Reproduction print; location of painting is unknown.
Courtesy of Private Collection

W. W. Denslow

The Other Wizard of Oz

Essay by Michael Patrick Hearn

The Exhibition
March 16 – May 19, 1996
Brandywine River Museum
Chadds Ford, Pennsylvania

This exhibition and publication was made possible,
in part, by a generous grant from the F. M. Kirby Foundation.

©1996 by the Brandywine Conservancy, Inc.
Essay © Michael Patrick Hearn
Library of Congress Catalogue number: 96-083578

Edited by Catherine E. Hutchins
Designed by Virginia H. O'Hara and Glenn Weiser
Photographs for the Brandywine River Museum by Rick Echelmeyer
Printed by Pearl Pressman Liberty Communications Group

Poster, Books to Burn!!
Courtesy of Columbia University Library

PREFACE

In its twenty-fifth year, as in 1971 with its first exhibition, the Brandywine River Museum celebrates American illustration. Through two and one-half decades, building on rich traditions engendered in the Brandywine valley, this Museum has presented the work of the best American illustrators. Is has done so by building collections of illustration and developing special exhibitions. We have stood firm — and been confirmed — in our belief that excellent illustration is often excellent art by any standard. As essays in many past exhibition catalogues testify, our curators have intently studied this area that too often has been ignored in the pursuit of art history. The present exhibition and publication continue that commitment. The Museum acquired its first Denslow work, "The Giant" from *Jack and the Bean-stalk,* as a gift from Jane Collette Wilcox in 1981. In 1994, it purchased a marvelous illustration titled "Long John Silver" used in Denslow's book, *The Pearl and the Pumpkin.* Thus, it is fitting that, as part of its silver anniversary events, the Museum examines and presents the career of W. W. Denslow, a strikingly original artist within the broad field of illustrators. Denslow was born in Philadelphia and, of course, is most often remembered as the first illustrator of L. Frank Baum's *The Wonderful Wizard of Oz.*

Michael Patrick Hearn, children's book critic and scholar who has intensely studied Denslow's life and work, initially suggested this undertaking. He is the extremely knowledgeable and ardent guest curator without whom this exhibition would not have occurred. We are grateful to Michael Patrick Hearn for his services, his consideration, and his important essay on the following pages.

Virginia H. O'Hara, associate curator of the Brandywine River Museum has an enduring interest in the artist. Her enthusiasm guided the development of this exhibition, its installation and its publication.

This publication was made possible, in part, by a generous grant from the F. M. Kirby Foundation which is due considerable gratitude for its continuing support of many museum programs.

Lenders to exhibitions make sacrifices so that others may enjoy and learn from the art they collected. Thus we thank the many individuals and institutions who have parted with original art, books and memorabilia in order that so much of W. W. Denslow's singular contribution to our culture can be studied here and now.

James H. Duff
Director

ACKNOWLEDGEMENTS

For their assistance in this undertaking, much appreciation is extended to Walter Albert; Robert A. Baum Jr.; Tom Beckman, Registrar, Historical Society of Delaware; Herman Bieber; Judy Bieber-Frietas; Bruce and Gail Crockett; Mark L. Denslow; Deborah Gangloff; Janet Tietjens Hart; C. Warren Hollister; Nina Manston; Patrick Maund; George Meredith; Fred M. Meyer; Gita Moreno; Wilson B. Roberts; Justin G. Schiller; Betsy B. Shirley; Mark Swartz; and the staffs of Butler Library, Columbia University; Shubert Archive; George Arents Research Library, Syracuse University; the New York Public Library; the Library of Congress; the Copyright Office; Notre Dame Archives, Notre Dame University; Circuit Court of Cook County Records, Chicago; and Emory University, Atlanta, Georgia.

Michael Patrick Hearn
Guest Curator

The Brandywine River Museum is indebted to Michael Patrick Hearn for suggesting this special project devoted to W. W. Denslow and for offering his considerable expertise in support of it. Mr. Hearn's knowledge of Denslow's life and career has increased appreciation for the artist's accomplishments and especially for his skill in design. We are also grateful to lenders Judy Bieber-Frietas; the Chapin Library of Rare Books, Williams College, Massachusetts; Chicago Historical Society; the de Grummond Collection, The University of Southern Mississippi, Hattiesburg; Bert and Ellen Denker; The Edith and C. Warren Hollister Oz Collection; Kerlan Collection, Children's Literature Research Collections, University of Minnesota; Beth and George Meredith; Fred M. Meyer; The Newberry Library, Chicago; Division of Prints and Photographs, The New York Public Library, Astor, Lenox and Tilden Foundations; Palmer Museum of Art, The Pennsylvania State University; Betsy B. Shirley, American Children's Literature Collection, Beinecke Library; Mrs. Andrew Wyeth, and anonymous lenders. Their generosity made this exhibition possible.

Virginia H. O'Hara
Associate Curator

Cat. 9 Old Bill Spear, Quincy, Mass. 1899

Cat. 68 Poster, *The Wonderful Wizard of Oz, 1900*

For Ozma Baum Mantele
M.P.H.

W. W. Denslow
The Other Wizard of Oz

Michael Patrick Hearn

...Who's this Denslow?
Who's this great and famous Denslow,
With the drooping fierce mustachio,
With the hippocampus ear-mark,
With the savage Jim Crow front on,
As of buccaneering days?
With the austere brow terrific,
With the flaming scarlet 'weskit,'
With the voice that growls and thunders,
And the pipe that ne'er goes out?

Paul Tietjens[1]

Who was W. W. Denslow? If he is remembered at all today, it is as the original illustrator of L. Frank Baum's *Wonderful Wizard of Oz* (1900). In his time he was also famous for *Denslow's Mother Goose* (1901), *Denslow's Night Before Christmas* (1902), and "Denslow's Picture Books for Children" (1903-4), but children's books constituted just a fraction of his total work. He was remarkably versatile as he effortlessly went from one area of commercial art to another. A pioneer in newspaper illustration, the art poster, the comic strip, and the picture book, he was also a skillful caricaturist and he designed remarkable stage sets and costumes. He helped establish the style and direction of Elbert Hubbard's Roycroft Shops. Denslow was an important American designer of the early twentieth century who has been largely ignored by scholars. His punchy, simple, ebullient style did much to steer American illustration away from the effusiveness and preciosity of the late Victorian age. While not an exceptional draftsman he had a manner all his own that was widely admired and freely imitated by his contemporaries. Denslow was not a great artist, but he was an extraordinary illustrator.

Denslow was also a man of contradictions. He was famous for his good spirits, his generosity, his hospitality, and his ferocity. He had quite a reputation as a ladies' man, and all of his three marriages ended in divorce. Poet Eunice Tietjens recalled him as "a delightful old reprobate who looked like a walrus."[2] Denslow the cynic made his name as a comic artist and filled jolly little designs for boys and girls with all sorts of happy, smiling characters. He became the most important American children's picture book artist of his time, but he abandoned his only son. This moody artist could be gregarious or querulous without warning. He was known for his wit and repartee, but not everyone appreciated his peculiar sense of humor. He was once described as "always grumbling about nothing, always carping, always censorious," yet laughing "uproariously when he had secured his effects."[3] He had many admirers and earned the respect of his peers, although he seems to have fought with nearly everyone he ever worked with. Of Denslow it could be truthfully said at times that he had no enemies, but none of his friends liked him. Of course not all the blame need be placed on his shoulders, for Denslow was hardly the only artist or writer of his age with an inflated ego. Indeed many of the people he worked with could be just as conceited and pig-headed. But arrogance is often a mask for insecurity. Although his books sold as well as they were reviewed, Denslow rarely received the critical recognition he so justly deserved. There was even strong hostility toward his work. At times the only thing that kept him going was his pride. Perhaps Eastern snobbery had something to do with the general neglect of his work. He never had the opportunity to study abroad, rarely exhibited his work, and did not mingle with the country's artistic elite. He also had the misfortune of making his name first in Chicago rather than in New York, Boston, or Philadelphia. He was a successful but minor artist until he began working with the equally obscure L. Frank Baum, and then these two men seemingly emerged out of nowhere to become the most inventive and influential people in America's children's books.

Despite the ensuing financial success, Denslow never joined the American publishing establishment. He placed little of his work with major houses, and only on occasion did his work appear in any of the leading national magazines like *Harper's Weekly, Harper's Bazar, Lippincott's, St. Nicholas, Life,* and *Cosmopolitan.* Instead he contributed to such ephemeral media as newspapers, trade journals, and advertisements. Denslow played the game by his own

William Wallace Denslow as a child, ca. 1859. Courtesy of the late Patricia Denslow Eykyn

rules. He considered himself an outsider and cultivated that position. His influence on modern children's book illustration may have been immense, but he was almost forgotten by the time of his death. His relative obscurity was in part his own fault. His violent mood swings might be diagnosed as manic-depressive today, but perhaps his erratic behavior can be traced to a life-long battle with alcoholism that eventually led to his death. Denslow's life and career like his temperament constituted a series of unpredictable highs and lows.

William Wallace Denslow, Jr., was born on May 5, 1856, in Philadelphia. "I don't know of any objection which can be urged against Philadelphia as a place in which to be born," he once said, "and I'm not ashamed to confess that I was introduced to earthly existence in the quiet old Quaker City. It makes a very respectable starting point. But this was all that Philadelphia afforded me, for my parents removed to Inwood-on-Hudson when I was an infant."[4] He was the second child of William Wallace and Jane Eva Evans Denslow. The family was apparently never prosperous and frequently moved as his father sought work. His mother was considered a beauty and one of the belles of New York. His brother Le Grand Norton was born in New York City in 1852, his sister Ethel Hayes in 1867 in Inwood; another sister, Eleanora Consuela, died only a few days short of her fourth birthday in 1864 in High Bridge, New York. William Wallace Denslow, Sr., had grown up on a farm near New

Haven, Connecticut. Family businesses included the manufacture of gun powder in Connecticut and the cotton trade in Georgia, but he seems to have gone out on his own into a variety of other professions—druggist, tobacconist, clerk, and botanist.

The part of childhood the younger Denslow remembered most affectionately was spent in Inwood on the northern tip of Manhattan, overlooking the Palisades. "In summer I rowed a skiff and in winter sailed an ice boat," he recalled. "Of course I would not today attempt the reckless and foolhardy ventures into which I threw all the energy of a healthy boy who was a stranger to fear of any sort. But now I don't regret a single one of the scrapes of those days, for I not only had a good a time as ever fell to the lot of boy, but I also unconsciously laid the foundation for a love of nature."[5] He also enjoyed drawing from an early age, filling copybooks with landscapes and animal studies. His father's first love was botany, and the boy sketched the floral specimens Denslow Sr. gathered on wanderings through the Hudson River Valley. Less appreciated were the boy's caricatures in the schoolroom on his slate and the blackboard. He had to do something to fight the boredom. "There was precious little printed then for a boy to laugh at," he later acknowledged, "and I made up my mind that some day I'd furnish the laugh material to them."[6]

He was only twelve when his father died. His brother went on to Columbia University to study medicine (and later became a noted genito-urinary specialist) while Denslow attended drawing classes in the Free

Night Schools of the Cooper Union for the Advancement of Science and Art between 1870 and 1872. One of his instructors William Magrath, a respected painter of Irish scenes, found him a job as office boy at Orange Judd Company, publishers of *American Agriculturist* and *Hearth and Home* magazines, where he learned the craft of drawing on the block for wood engraving, then the most popular form of reproduction. His earliest work appeared in these periodicals; however, much of it was uninspired unsigned cuts of chicken coops, bird houses, cooking stoves, ice cream freezers, prize fruit, and the like. At that time the children's page of *Hearth and Home* was edited by Mary Mapes Dodge and her assistant Frank R. Stockton (later the author of "The Lady or the Tiger?"). Dodge was the first to recognize Denslow's ability as an illustrator for young readers and published some of his novice work, generally simple rebuses. When she founded *St. Nicholas,* the greatest of all children's magazines, she included another of Denslow's picture puzzles in an early issue.

Denslow was fortunate in meeting many illustrators both at school and as they passed through Orange Judd: James Kelly famous for his horse drawings; Edwin Forbes for his Civil War sketches; and William Hamilton Gibson for his botanical studies; the Beard brothers, James Carter, Frank, and Dan; Mike Woolf for his sketches of slum urchins. They all generously offered Denslow pointers on how to improve his work. He was also lucky his first semester at school to be among those invited to the attic studio of sculptor Jonathon Scott Hartley. That

Portrait of W.W. Denslow, ca. 1910. Courtesy of Fred M. Meyer night in November 1871, they decided to form a sketch class that eventually developed into the famous Salmagundi Club. Their first meeting included painter Will H. Low and cartoonist Fred S. Church as well as "Billie" Denslow. Bohemians all, they took a vow of poverty to keep their group free of the pretensions that afflicted other artists' organizations. Each week they chose a subject, and on the following Saturday, they tacked up their drawings on Hartley's big easel for criticism. Afterwards they spent the rest of the evening chatting, boxing or fencing. Denslow hardly had to promise to remain a poor starving artist, for he was just barely surviving. Once when a wealthy friend asked him to house-sit while he was in Europe, Denslow had to walk across town because he could not afford the fare, and he subsisted on a big can of corn meal that happened to have been left behind.

Denslow progressed well enough in his studies at Cooper Union to transfer to the National Academy of Design. Here he took instruction in the "antique," in which he worked from plaster casts of classical sculpture, and he went on to "life" drawing where he sketched the clothed model. He lasted

barely three years. His formal art training abruptly ended at age eighteen when his mother remarried in 1874 and moved to Newburgh, New York. Thus Denslow remained largely self-taught. He learned best by doing. Whatever he lacked in technical expertise, he often made up for in energy and humor. He left Orange Judd about 1876 for a better paying position on the art staff of the recently founded New York *Daily Graphic,* the first American pictorial newspaper. The paper encouraged anonymity by establishing an assembly line for artists; one might do the figures, another the buildings, a third the animals. William Allen Rogers, Edward Windsor Kemble, and Charles Jay Taylor were all there the same time he was, but no illustrations signed "Denslow" have been found in its pages.

Had he had more training, Denslow's career might have gone in quite another direction. Like many of his contemporaries, he viewed Edwin Austin Abbey and Charles Stanley Reinhart as the artists who "first awakened the art of illustrating in America from a long Rip Van Winkle trance-like sleep." In Denslow's estimation, "They were the new pioneers in the new illustrative art of today.

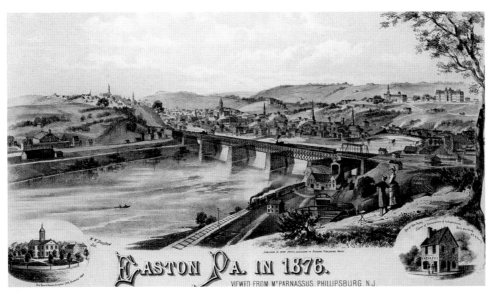

Cat. 57
Easton, Pennsylvania, in 1876 viewed from Mt. Parnassus, Phillipsburg, N.J., 1876.
Courtesy of the Palmer Museum of Art, Pennsylvania State University

With them it made a bond that places the American illustrator upon the high artistic level he occupies."[7] They elevated illustration into a fine art and founded a new school of magazine illustration. Although many artists, such as Abbey, John LaFarge, Childe Hassam, and Winslow Homer, used illustration merely as a stepping stone to careers in painting, Denslow devoted his life almost exclusively to commercial art. He is not known to have worked in oils, and not many watercolors by him survive. W. W. Denslow was a line man, not a painter, and he drew primarily for reproduction. He knew the limitations of printing processes and adapted his style to meet their requirements.

By nature Denslow was a comic artist, and he never harbored the ambitions and pretensions of either an Abbey or a Reinhart. The illustrator who perhaps most notably influenced his art in the early years was True W. Williams, Mark Twain's chief collaborator. Denslow's 1870s sketches have the same stiff, cramped drawing style and squat figures with limited expressions, poses, and gestures that are in Williams' pictures for Twain's *Sketches New and Old* (1875), and *The Adventures of Tom Sawyer* (1876). Coincidentally Denslow was just one of many artists (including Williams) who contributed to Twain's *A Tramp Abroad* (1880), but Denslow's debt to Williams is most obvious in the drawings for George M. Hayes' pamphlet *Twenty Years on the Road* (1884).

Denslow could not be choosy about what work to take, and he was not proud of everything he did do. Perhaps the most alarmingly ubiquitous of his early commissions was an advertisement for a chewing tobacco. "I turned out what I considered a fair job," he recalled, "and then I forgot all about it. Shortly after, however, I made a trip through the New England states, and wherever I went I was confronted by that tobacco sign. At first I was rather pleased at seeing my handiwork so profusely displayed, but soon I began to see the defects in my work—and I may acknowledge now that they were many and glaring. I grew to detest this particular showcard, and the more I saw of it the more repugnant it became. But I found I could not escape it. At the hotel, the barber shop, the grocery—even on the fences—this horrid example of crude art stared me in the face." It haunted him for years. No matter what part of the country he was in, it was there. "In a hut up in the Rockies a miner had posted my tobacco card," he said. "A cowpuncher on a Colorado ranch had the horror stuck up in the back of his shed." He eventually had to admit that "the thing was not so bad, but it was bad enough to make my life miserable for a number of years, and if you want to send a cold shiver down my back just ask me to make a showcard for chewing tobacco!"[8] When interviewed, he never identified which tobacco ad it was.

In 1876 Denslow left the *Daily Graphic* for the chance to wander about Maine. His friend Charles W. Waldron was then the proprietor and salesman for a patent medicine and asked him to come along to help him paint rocks, trees, barns, and fences with one message: "Use Wing's Pills." Denslow's "hale-fellow-well-met, go-as-you-please-air and picturesque humor . . . found expression in many an ingenuous way and created amusement wherever he went."[9] The two encountered plenty of adventure along the way. Once while blithely walking down a country road, they met a great black bear who sent them scurrying back where they came from. Another time they happened upon a cow with a board across her horns; while Waldron held the beast, Denslow painted not only the plank but her flanks as well. The two thoroughly enjoyed themselves during their travels, fishing when they could and on occasion giving "chalk talks" in small country towns.

With the arrival of cooler weather, Denslow left for Philadelphia to see the centennial celebration, but he was soon on the road again. The nation's hundredth anniversary launched a wave of civic pride, and lithographers sent Denslow across Pennsylvania, New York, and Maryland, to draw images for the spate of county atlases and local histories. He sketched rural landmarks and made bird's-eye views of various towns, and soon he mastered the art of drawing directly on the stone. These lithographs, often issued hand-colored, were no better and no worse than the countless other prints then on the market all over the country, but Denslow found it uninspiring, frustrating work because farmers demanded that he draw their homesteads not as they were but as they wanted them to look. Feeling he was being robbed by his employers, Denslow quit and returned to Philadelphia.

Eager for any work he could find, Denslow teamed with another artist Edward W. Woodard on fashionable Chestnut Street. Their design studio was right in the heart of the theater district, so much of its work was done for the stage. This was the heyday of traveling companies that needed broadsides, flyers, and an assortment of advertisements they could carry from town to town to drum up business for evening performances. Most of this work was either unsigned or faintly marked "W. D." Denslow produced gaudily lithographed posters and trade cards primarily for the printers Thomas Sinclair & Son and Baker & Hayes, both of Philadelphia, promoting long-forgotten productions like the Hanlon Brothers in *Le Voyage en Suisse,* McCaull Opera Comique Company's *Falka* and *Beggar Prince,* Harrison and Gourlay's *Skipped by the Light of the Moon,* and Salsbury's Troubadours' *Three of a Kind.* To ensure that he accurately captured the poses and the lighting, Denslow often sketched from the audience during performances. On occasion he designed costumes for shows. Yet times were still difficult for the young artist. Eager to see a Henry Irving performance, Denslow and some friends tried to squeeze tickets out of the actor by sending him an elaborate request illustrated with a drawing of themselves out in the snow looking longingly at a poster of Irving and Ellen Terry in *Twelfth Night.* The star was so amused and flattered by their effort that he provided them with a full week's supply of box seats during the Philadelphia run.[10]

It was in Philadelphia that Denslow met Annie McCartney, the daughter of a stable proprietor, and it did not take much for the snappily dressed young artist with the walrus mustache to win her heart. They were married on November 30, 1882, and she bore him a son William Wallace Jr., his only child, on November 1, 1883. The Denslows, however, were not compatible. It is likely his drinking aggravated the situation. On August 20, 1884, Annie left their home with the boy out of "voluntary perverse-

Cat. 65
Poster
The
Marbeau
Cousins,
1898

ness" (or so Denslow said).[11] Being a devout Irish Catholic, she refused to divorce him and her father took responsibility for the child. Denslow and his wife briefly corresponded in 1886, but that was their last direct communication. He never saw her or his son again.

Denslow and another artist Charles W. Lemon went into partnership on Sansom Street and produced all kinds of ephemera. Sometimes the partners signed their own names and at others used the signature "W. D. & L." They did flyers, calendar cards, magazines covers, and cartoons as well as pamphlets like *Order of the Day in Camp* (1885) and *Mrs. Brown's Opinions* (1885). In 1885 they left for New York City to open another studio. They roomed together in Croton-on-Hudson but quickly parted company. Lemon remembered Denslow as "a bright, showy fellow, but . . . a cad, vain and good looking with snappy black eyes and a big brown mustache. He must have had sex appeal, because I heard that he stole the wives of three other artists. . . . He was flashy, but he did not wear well anywhere." Lemon went so far as to call him "a son of a bitch."[12]

On his own, Denslow drew portraits, cartoons, and scenes from shows for *The Theatre.* In 1888 he drifted into the relatively new profession of newspaper illustration, working primarily for the American Press Association. When Joseph Pulitzer added pictures to the New York *World* in the 1880s, circulation of that daily increased tremendously; soon other newspapers were scrambling to hire artists. Few of Denslow's drawings survive from this period because the newspaper artist like an etcher worked directly on a plate. It was a cumbersome, impractical process at first and demanded simplicity and economy in execution. (Newspaper illustrators were called "chalk scratchers" because their steel plates were coated with a preparation of chalk and adhesive. Once the image was drawn on the plate a hand bellows sent the loose chalk dust flying everywhere.) Space for pictures in the papers was highly restricted. Only thumbnail sketches, no bigger than a square inch or two, were generally required, and the printed images were often crude, blurred, and indistinct. Nonetheless Denslow always seemed to find a clear and obvious spot for his signature "Den." When zincography was introduced to the daily paper, a larger pen drawing could be photographed, reduced, and reproduced with some reasonable fidelity to the original, but the lines had to be sharp and precise to be picked up by the camera and then by the plate. According to Denslow, all newspaper artists' work suffered from "bad printing, worse paper and the destroying angel, the photoengraver with his all-powerful routing machine, whereby he puts to route the best of artistic efforts (hence its name), eyes, buttons and fingers vanish before it, even decapitation comes within the execution of this dread machine when wielded by that midnight fiend, the newspaper engraver."[13]

Denslow altered his methods to fit the limitations of the medium. His drawing became simpler, stronger, and generally devoid of superfluous line or detail. Style was subservient to subject. His drawings had to "read" as easily as the reports they illustrated. Aside from newspaper work, Denslow did pictures for Henry M. Hunt's *Crime of the Century* (1889), J. P. Johnston's *Twenty Years of Hus'ling* (1889), and P. T. Barnum's memoir *Dollars and Sense* (1890), which also included some early drawings by Will H. Bradley. These line drawings were hardly an improvement on what Denslow had been supplying the papers, and they caused no special notice for him as a book illustrator.

In 1887 Denslow met James W. Scott, who invited him to work for his pro-Democrat journal the

Chicago *Herald.* Curious about life in the Midwest, Denslow took him up on the offer. It was the Golden Age of Chicago journalism. Eugene Field, Peter Finley Dunne, Brand Whitlock, George Ade, and John T. McCutcheon were just a few of the men now making names for themselves in that city's numerous newspapers. Denslow met them at the Press Club of Chicago and the notorious Whitechapel Club. The latter group, taking their name from the area of London in which the Jack the Ripper murders occurred, had decorated the rear of a saloon near the *Herald* building with a card table made out of a coffin, gas lamps and tobacco jars out of human skulls, and gruesome trophies as murder weapons, nooses from executions, and bloody blankets from the Dakotas. Although never an official member of the club, Denslow felt right at home drinking and carrying on among all these macabre mementos.

More than ever alcohol was disrupting Denslow's work. After reportedly being fired several times for insobriety on the job, he found the courage to take the radical "Keeley Cure," and left for the Keeley Institute in Dwight, Illinois, to take a series of injections of double chloride of gold that were believed to be remarkably effective against the disease. Denslow's reputation was so tarnished in Chicago, that afterwards he thought it best to see something of frontier life. He left for Denver to work for the *Rocky Mountain News.* As head of this pro-Democrat paper's art department, Denslow drew everything from political cartoons to want ads. But the tenderfoot was not prepared for Colorado politics in action. While covering the local Republican convention, he became convinced that every man, woman, and child was armed with a six-shooter pointed in his direction and dove under the table for cover.

After two months he quarreled with his boss and quit. Then he set off for the cattle range. "No sooner did I find my first employment as a cow puncher than I was convinced that this was the kind of existence for which I had always had a vague and indefinite longing," he said.[14] He did have an unpleasant encounter with his horse. It appeared so meek and skinny at first that Denslow was certain that no harm could ever come to its rider. All went well until one day without provocation the horse bucked and threw him to the ground. Later Denslow was grateful for the ornery beast when a pack of hungry timber wolves chased them back to the ranch house. When the glamour of home on the range paled, the artist briefly tried mining, and then he headed for San Francisco to return to newspaper work.

Eventually Denslow worked for most of the leading papers in the city, the *Call,* the *Chronicle,* and the *Examiner,* as well as the *Wasp* and *California Illustrated Magazine.* Even in eccentric San Francisco, Denslow was considered a character. "Mr. Denslow is as erratic a mortal as ever blossomed into the West," the *Call* reported, "and as a newspaper caricaturist he has few rivals. . . . Denslow is not only a rapid worker, but his clean, sharp lines are the delight of the zincographer, who never fears a spoiled plate when 'Den' is in good trim." With his big bushy mustache and pointed beard, wide-brimmed hats and big bow ties, "Den's' personal appearance readily lends itself to caricature."[15] However amusing he may have seemed to others, Denslow was miserable. He felt persecuted by his colleagues and frustrated with his work: "This world is a great one," he grumbled, "and lately seems to me to be built on the joke principle, and as usual the joke is on me. It always has been and I suspect it always will be even to my deathbed. In my last moment I suspect that someone will give it to me in the neck and perhaps get ahead of me with St. Peter."[16]

He was covering the theater, politics, trials, and executions, but "almost my entire time was spent sketching in Chinatown," he later recalled. "This I regard as perhaps the most valuable and interesting experience that ever came to me. I saw the most exciting conflicts between the Highbinders and their victims, and followed the police on their raids." He hoped to do a book on Chinatown, and meanwhile he cultivated his taste for the beauties of Asian art by collecting fans, screens, crockery, toys, and whatever else he could find, having determined that "the Chinese, like the Japanese, . . . [are a] wonderfully artistic people in a decorative sense."[17] Their art profoundly influenced Denslow's work, and he increasingly worked their principles of decoration into his illustrations.

While on the *Examiner's* staff, Denslow asked the publisher William Randolph Hearst to bankroll a trip back to Chicago to cover the 1893 World's Columbian Exposition. Hearst refused, so Denslow and fellow artist Charles W. Saalburg quit and departed for Chicago anyway. Denslow was ready for a change. "It is no Golden West," he groused. "There are more unemployed and poverty-stricken people in comparison to the population than any other city I know of. And more deviltry among the few who have money. The city of San Francisco is rank and rotten to the core."[18] He, like so

many of his contemporaries, believed the World's Fair made Chicago the place to be. He and Saalburg opened an office in the Chicago *Post* building. But as in so many instances before, he and his partner soon had a row and went their separate ways. Denslow became the *Herald's* chief artist and Saalburg was soon the competing *Inter-Ocean's* principal political cartoonist.

At first Denslow was as critical of Chicago as he had been of San Francisco: "A more disgusting place than the stockyards can scarcely be imagined. . . . It is simply vile."[19] But Chicago welcomed Denslow back. The *Herald* gave him plenty of work at a good salary and let him do any other illustrating he wanted to on the side. The paper sent him and reporter Leroy Armstrong to check on the fair's progress and produce a series of articles for the Sunday edition. One of the most impressive sights was the construction of the first Ferris Wheel. "When we got under the wheel and looked aloft," he noted in his diary, "my courage oozed out the holes in my socks. I flatly refused to climb so they made a sling or a bowline, as they called it, and proceeded to hoist us by steam power. . . . I have been on Pike's and other peaks but never so high as it appeared to me on that bloomin' wheel."[20] He called down to Armstrong, "Now if the good Lord only

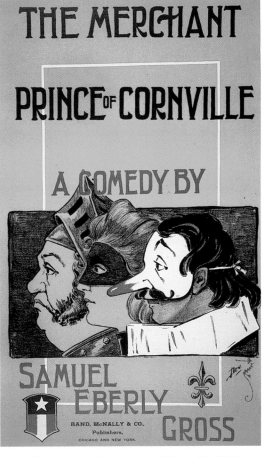

Cat. 59 Poster, Merchant Prince of Cornville, 1895

permits me to get back to earth again in safety, I promise you to stick to that level forever after, if I never make another picture. Say, but I don't like this!"[21] Safely back on the ground, the two visited all the other sights and attractions of the great Columbian Exposition, most notably the opening of the fair itself and Buffalo Bill's Wild West Show. Denslow found the exposition exhilarating. "It is literally stunning, the immensity of the thing. Miles of ground covered with tremendous and artistic buildings. My first thoughts were, knowing that they are only intended for short use of six months, was what a magnificent ruin they must make when all is finished."[22] He did indeed have himself photographed among the ruins at its close. Nothing ever came of the World's Fair book he had planned to do with Saalburg, but he and Armstrong did burlesque reactions to the exposition in *Byrd Flamm in Town* (1894), which they initially published in the *Herald.*

Chicago grew into an art center of international importance as painters and sculptors came from all over the world to attend the fair. The artist who most profoundly influenced Denslow was British cartoonist Phil May, then covering the exposition for the London *Daily Graphic.* "I will take my hat off to him," Denslow later recalled, "his humor was of the American rather than the English order. It didn't take a surgical operation to get a joke into Phil May's head."[23] Denslows' immediate admiration for May's work is evident in the American's sketchy line and economic comic characterization in his newspaper work.

The fair provided another important stimulus to his art. Denslow's first thoughts, when told to cover Carl Hegenback's famous trained animal act from Hamburg, were, "Ye gods! What will I do with the same?"[24] However, the assignment proved to be a revelation. There he noticed how intelligent bears

Cat. 76 Cover design and lettering for *Lorna Doone,* 1897. Courtesy of the Chapin Library, Williams College

were, how expressive was the elephant's face. In "Crafty Wild Beasts" (May 14), Denslow first explored in any depth the possibilities of giving human expressions to animals through comparative anatomy, a technique that came in handy when he began illustrating children's books.

After the fair closed, work for the *Herald* was steady but unchallenging. "I float, as it were, with the stream," Denslow informed a cousin in early 1895, "enjoying life as I float. I *do* have a good time and make no mistake, besides that I work very hard, being at it night and day."[25] All that changed by year's end. When James W. Scott purchased the *Times* and consolidated it with the *Herald* as the Chicago *Times-Herald* on March 4, 1895, Denslow designed the handsome poster that advertised the event. But then Scott died, and wealthy businessman Herman H. Kohlsaat, an aggressive supporter of William McKinley, purchased the staunchly Democratic paper. Despite Kohlsaat's initial promises of noninterference, the *Times-Herald* became more and more Republican; editors, reporters, and artists fled to rival papers.

Denslow realized that it was time to turn free-

W.W. Denslow viewing the
demolition of World's Columbian
Exposition, ca. 1893.
Courtesy of the Library of Congress.

lance, but it was a tough decision. "When one gets to be a newspaperman," he confessed, "it is much like a disease, hard to get out of. Of course, I should like to do something better, but a big salary and solid comfort make one hesitate to lean to something else; besides I am well thought of where I am, no one dictates to me, having my own studio, the door which I can keep locked for one week's end to another if I liked."[26] Once he quit the paper Denslow was free to contribute to the *Times-Herald, Chronicle,* and any of the city's other papers. He published for the short-lived Chicago humor magazine *Uncle Sam,* and some slightly racy drawings appeared in the *Echo,* a lightweight *fin-de-siècle* fortnightly. Taking advantage of a current bicycle craze, Denslow provided picture puzzles for a bicycle contest that the *Times-Herald* sponsored in the summer of 1895 as well as designs for *Wheel Talk,* a specialty journal. He also exhibited work in the "Black and White Show" of the Chicago Society of Artists and "The Century and Echo Poster Show," for which exhibitions he also designed the catalogue covers.

The most challenging commission to follow Denslow's immediate departure from the *Times-Herald* was designing all the costumes for *Little Robinson Crusoe,* a Harry B. Smith musical burlesque starring Eddie Foy and Marie Dressler. The lavish summer production at Chicago's Schiller Theatre required his clothing troupes of marines, sailors, pirates, bell boys, fairies, cannibals, a parrot, and a green-whiskered goat. (Denslow went off to Chicago's Hawthorne Racetrack to get the jockey outfits just right for the chorus girls in a racy racing number.) Foy alone had six changes of costume. In all Denslow provided fifty watercolors for the clothes and color effects and designed the play's large lithographed poster.

What made Denslow one of Chicago's most important commercial artists was his substantial contribution to the international artistic poster movement then sweeping the country. Perhaps nowhere did the principles of the arts and crafts movement in bringing fine art to the people find their most effective expression than in the turn-of-the century art poster. The fad originated with Frenchman Jules Chéret who for years had been brightening Paris streets with gaudy lithographs promoting music halls, cabarets, and other entertain-

ments. He was soon joined by Henri Toulouse-Lautrec, Eugène Grasset, Alphonse Mucha, Théophile Steinlen, Georges de Feure, and many others who brought their distinctive styles to these cheap prints. England answered with Aubrey Beardsley's eccentric sensuous black and white designs, William Nicholson and James Pryde's Beggarstaff Brothers paper cutouts, and Dudley Hardy's and John Hassall's lively theatrical ads. In America Will H. Bradley, Edward Penfield, Louis J. Rhead, Ethel Reed, Maxfield Parrish, and Joseph C. Leyendecker designed primarily for magazines, newspapers, and books. There was also Jan Toorop in Amsterdam, Thomas Theodore Heine in Munich, and Gustav Klimt and Berthold Löffler in Vienna. These often wild, uninhibited broadsides were collected and discussed all over the world and revolutionized both advertising and illustration.

A poster does not speak, it shouts. Its message must be loud and clear to catch the attention of the indifferent passerby. Therefore artists relied on the unexpected to get their meaning across while keeping the pictures as simple and economical as possible. Denslow was no exception.[27] He relearned how to compose a picture to make his announcements as immediate and memorable as possible. Japanese and

Chinese precepts were challenging Western traditions, and poster artists eagerly adopted the two dimensional manner to their advertisements and abandoned one-point perspective, conventional light and shade, exact form and proportion, and correct anatomy. Compositions were broken down to their elements and then reconstructed. Form was reduced to a sensuous, serpentine outline, space to a flat backdrop. Figures were flooded in bright artificial light, and color was used for visual effect rather than to reflect reality. It is no surprise that the more bizarre designs were ridiculed for their blue faces, impossible bodies, and snake-like locks. Art for art's sake had never been quite like this before.

Because speed and economy demanded there be no more than three colors for a poster, Denslow learned to make the most of the least. Sometimes he avoided black altogether, which was remarkable because Denslow generally drew in India ink only. He worked closely with the printers to determine which color mixtures to use and make sure that they performed exactly as he wished. He soon found out what could and could not be done with contemporary methods of reproduction. He extended the ranges of hue and tone by overlapping the colors and introducing a variety of benday screens. He made effective use of the white of the page, and at other times he had his designs printed on tinted paper. The results were indeed startling and not at all naturalistic. Like other poster artists, Denslow introduced color for its own sake. He played with harmony and contrast in these cheaply produced but still attractive prints. He also experimented with lettering, coming up with a remarkable variety of styles that he (unlike some of his contemporaries) always kept clear and legible.

One could always tell a Denslow poster by his distinctive totem worked somewhere on the composition. The economy and utility of advertisements demanded that less was more, and all the other "copy" generally left little room for a full signature; indeed, sometimes an artist's signature could throw off the composition. Accordingly many poster designers had to be content with remaining anonymous. Not W. W. Denslow. He came up with an easily recognizable identifying device. J. M. Whistler had his barbed butterfly; Walter Crane had a Japanese crane; and Denslow had his hippocampus (sea horse). He confided to friend and photographer Alfred Stieglitz, "It is well to have a sign or a totem, as my hippocampus has saved many a composition for me, and I hold him in reserve for that purpose."[28] Denslow had first used it in San Francisco on occasional pictures, but after 1895 rarely did a design ever leave his home without it. So identifiable was he to his symbol that Denslow became known among artists as "Hippocampus Den."

Although such important painters as Toulouse-Lautrec, Pierre Bonnard, and Félix Vallottin were turning to "the poor man's art gallery," thus helping to erase the lines between high and low art, Denslow had never had any use for such arbitrary distinctions. Once when a friend protested that he knew nothing about art to give his opinion of Denslow's work, the artist laughed and said, "Neither does the public; that's why I want your viewpoint."[29] As far as Denslow was concerned, art was just art. He freely borrowed elements from his colleagues' work. His earliest posters owed much to Chéret's famous placards, but the Frenchman's influence soon gave way to a variety of sources, notably English designers Dudley Hardy and John Hassall.

Denslow also collected posters and quickly became one of Chicago's most knowledgeable connoisseurs of the new art form. In 1896 and 1897 he even wrote the monthly column "Poster Art" for the *Bill Poster,* a trade journal for printers. His erudite commentary covered what was happening in Chicago, New York, Paris, London, Vienna, Munich, and St. Petersburg. He could be quite caustic: "a great mass of the stuff we see, even from the hands of the good men of the old guard, are as bald of ideas, as a pig that has shot the chutes at Armour's is innocent of bristles."[30] He had little patience with current excesses and eccentricities: "the reckless putting out of poster hieroglyphics, which no one understands." And he could be sarcastic, as when he decried the efforts of Beardsley, Bradley, or their lesser imitators whose work appeared to be "the illuminated ravings of some incompetent dope fiend, who neglected to educate himself before he took to the pipe and poppy."[31] What he thought most wanting in contemporary posters was "a little comedy. . . . Why not liven the poster up a bit with merry jibe or jest? The poster maker is too much in earnest, too somber. Give us some side splitters."[32]

In 1896 Denslow's clever parody of Will H. Bradley's highly stylized "Twins," the poster advertising the March 1895 *Chap-Book,* showed what could be done. For the Chicago *Times-Herald,* Denslow produced "Imitation of a Newsboy Selling the Herald to a Haughti Lady," which sported a serpentine woman as contemptuous as he thought Bradley's "Twins" were and a newsboy cribbed from Beardsley. (He repeated the joke as "The Haughty Sisters Shopping," the December 1899 picture for the poster calendar issued by Chicago Photo-Engraving Company.) The burlesque immediately became Denslow's most famous poster and was reprinted everywhere. "There is only one thing that is unfortunate, which is my own fault," he admitted. "When I made the 'Haughti Lady'. . . I tried to imitate Bradley's style and caricature it, as joke on Bradley who is a very near friend of mine.

In so doing I also copied his signature to the extent of signing myself 'Will W. Denslow.' It is the only time I ever did it, but every one from the Atlantic to the Pacific seems to have seen it and whenever my name appears in print it is as 'Will W.'"[33] In England he was called "Wilfred Denslow."

Denslow provided his column "free of charge," for (as the editor of the magazine reminded him) "you are the gainer by having your poster sketches advertised in a paper of as wide a circulation as the *Bill Poster*," and boosted his own career and those of such up-and-coming artists as Edward Penfield, Maxfield Parrish, and Ike Morgan, the last being a young *Times-Herald* cartoonist with whom Denslow for a time shared his studio. He even promoted friends who were not poster designers. But he soon grew disillusioned with the *Bill Poster* because the editors failed to sell sketches they had commissioned from him, and they refused to give back the originals. "You have an idea that every man should pay tribute to Denslow," was one editor's caustic reply to his repeated requests for their return, "and I believe that I am about the only man alive who has ever gotten any charitable work from you, and I flatter myself that you have been ten fold repaid the good the *Bill Poster* has done you."[34] But Denslow did not see it that way, and he brought suit against the journal.

The great majority of Denslow's posters advertised books issued by Rand McNally, then one of the Midwest's largest publishers of popular literature (in addition to maps and atlases). Denslow graduated from advertising the titles to adorning their covers with "flat, decorative designs, thus making every publication a poster unto itself."[35] Publishers were constantly repackaging old literature in new dress, and most of the cloth bindings Denslow designed were for reprints. As it was years before pictorial dust jackets came into general use, books were indeed judged by their covers, so their bindings had to be bright, brash, and sometimes even eccentric to snare the eye of the fickle customer. "The influence of the broad effective poster," Denslow noted, "has been beneficial . . . on both paper and cloth book covers . . . and in wandering through a store . . . one is struck by the many beautiful things he sees on cloth books that are traced directly to the influence of the poster."[36] Preferring to do work that was "out of the rut and clearly up to date," Denslow was soon acknowledged as one of the masters of the new decorative art.[37]

There were even more restrictions on a designer of book covers than on the poster artist. Color and economy were everything. Because the cloth was stamped with only a few stencils, Denslow had to rely less on line than on large flat masses of color. Subtlety in drawing was sacrificed to minimal compositions dependant on tonal harmonies. These had to be emblematic as well as ornamental, for they did not illustrate as much as suggest or define the character of the book's content. These limitations further refined Denslow's color sense, and he produced numerous covers, many of which have a tiny sea horse worked somewhere into the composition. The best of these remain fine examples of American art nouveau.

Denslow next designed covers for paperbacks. The railroads had created a demand for cheap reading that could be hawked in the stations and on the cars. Rand McNally offered these "butcher boy books" in their successful Globe Library, Oriental Library, and Rialto Series, and Denslow provided a vast number of unusual covers for their lists. The influence of the art poster is even more evident on these paperbacks than it was on the hardcovers. His often graceful, sometimes alarming designs succeeded in selling more than a few volumes of dubious literary value to distracted commuters. The line was comprised primarily of 25¢ westerns, thrillers, and other sensational fiction, both reprints and originals by Richard Henry Savage, Marie Corelli, Leroy Armstrong, Hal Caine, and many others. Because Denslow poured out a steady stream of more than one hundred designs in slightly over two years, the quality varied. But on the whole, these are as striking as his book posters. In some cases he used the same design for both purposes.

About 1893 Denslow joined the Chicago Press Club, where he solidified his position within the city's publishing industry. Here he met Opie Read, a popular writer of regional humor whose *A Tennessee Judge* (1893) and *A Tear in a Cup and Other Stories* (1894) Denslow illustrated. Unfortunately Denslow's contributions to Read's rustic fiction were undistinguished black-and-white wash drawings, then the fashion but lacking the finesse and character of his line work. Far better were the textual pictures Denslow and Ike Morgan did for Read's *Arkansas Planter* (1896) that Rand McNally published. To capture the appropriate atmosphere in his ink drawings, Denslow spent six weeks sketching in the cotton

Cat. 61 Poster, Imitation of a Newsboy Selling the Herald to a Haughti Lady, 1896

fields and cyprus swamps of Arkansas. The book's poster too was Denslow's work, and he went on to provide the covers for Read's paperback novels *Mrs. Annie Green* (1898) and *Up Terrapin River* (1898) in the Globe Library as well as those for *The Waters of Caney Fork* (1898) and *A Yankee from the West* (1898) in hardcover.

Another of Denslow's dearest friends on newspaper row was Martha Jane Everts Holden, the "Queen of Bohemia." "That great and good pure woman" was one of the city's most respected journalists and signed her work in the *Herald* under the name "Amber" after the color of her hair.[38] Publisher Scott had said that her columns brought more letters to the editor than any of the paper's other features. Being a woman, she could not join either the Chicago Press Club or the Whitechapel Club, therefore she founded the Bohemian Club which briefly flourished as a haven for the city's growing artistic community. Among Holden's protégées was the young dancer Isadora Duncan, who

Will Bradley (1868-1962) Cover for *The Chap Book,* 1894

thought the Bohemians "the most surprising group of people—poets, artists, and actors of every nationality. They only seemed to have one thing in common: they were all without a cent." At their Tuesday meetings there was Amber in the thick of it, "calling in a voice like a man's: 'All good Bohemians rally round! All good Bohemians rally round!' And every time she called the Bohemians to rally round, they lifted their beer mugs and responded with cheers and songs."[39] For the door of the club in the Boyce Building, Denslow provided an appropriate stained glass design: a writer's pen, an artist's palette, and an actor's mask.

But it was less Amber than her pretty daughter Ann Waters Holden, a skilled writer in her own right, who attracted Denslow. Her mother's name for the sunny blonde was "Blossom," humorist George Ade called her Ann "Sparkling" Waters, and Denslow often used her as a model for his pictures. When Amber suddenly died of cancer in early 1895, it was Denslow who came to the family's aid by editing and arranging for publication two collections of Amber's columns in book form—*Rosemary and Rue* (1896) and *Amber Glints* (1897)—to benefit her son Hoyt's education, and by designing the books' covers and posters. Ann Waters was eternally grateful to her "Pirate" (as she called him), "for he came to her when she was in sorrow and in need of just such a loyal friend and advisor."[40] Although she was nearly twenty years his junior, Denslow asked her to marry him. There was just the small problem of a wife back in Philadelphia, so Denslow sent his lawyer to check on Annie McCartney Denslow. He learned that for at least five months she had been living with one Oscar Low as his wife, and under the name "Mrs. Anna Low" had charged him with assault. On September 6, 1895, Denslow filed for divorce on the grounds of adultery, and won his

release on February 20, 1896. That very day he and Ann Waters went to Milwaukee to get married.

With a pretty new wife and now relatively prosperous, the nearly forty-year-old Bohemian exuded a reasonable degree of respectability as he entered his prime as a commercial artist. Leroy Armstrong described Denslow about that time: "A shortish man, with a stocky frame, capable of trouble in the old days, and toughened by many seasons. He doesn't wear long hair, nor wander about in velveteen. Indeed, he is an extremely orderly person, with pens and pencils all company front, and portfolios full of classified, indexed matter. He has a dress suit, and is regarded as sufficiently conventional. . . . He has a bankbook, and is the hardest trader that ever dabbled camel's hair brush in chrome yellow. If it wasn't for his pictures he wouldn't pass for an artist at all."[41] Denslow and his young bride moved to the suburb of Highwood, where they found a comfortable house built on a bluff overlooking Lake Michigan. Painting his sea horse logo on the front door, he christened the place "Hippocampus," and he and Ann Waters made their home as

Cat. 63 Poster, Why Travel?, ca. 1896

inviting as possible for their many friends.

One of the people Denslow had met through Amber was writer Charles Warren Stoddard from California, and the two collaborated on a collection of Near Eastern travel sketches, *A Cruise under the Crescent* (1898) that Rand McNally published. This was the most ambitious book assignment Denslow had yet received, and he filled it with all sorts of lively marginalia. Stoddard stayed with the Denslows while working on the project. "We cannot see the lake, for the grove that stands between," Stoddard described Hippocampus, "but I can hear it, and walk to [the] bluff and back in three minutes! The trees are full of song birds and the garden of flowers. My writing-window looks north down into a ravine filled with trees."[42] He also accompanied the Denslows and other friends from the press on a trip up Lake Superior to Marquette, Michigan, where they founded "The Tribe of Scribes of the So-Sa-Wa-Ga-Ming Club of Yellow Dog River." Stoddard was so taken with the natural beauties of the area that he wrote "The Art-Gallery of the Great Lakes," which was illustrated by Denslow and published in the September 1899 issue of *Cosmopolitan.*

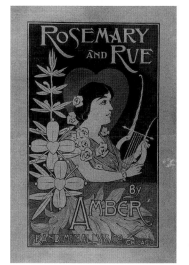

Cat. 62 Poster, Rosemary and Rue, 1896

Denslow for once seemed relatively content with his life. "An easy chair, a long, cool pipe, well seasoned, the Arcadia Mixture, and good, rare old books," he mused. "Say, what more do you want?"[43] His new prosperity allowed him to become an avid bibliophile, and he filled his bookcases at Highwood with fine first and deluxe editions. In 1896, when he ordered a copy of *The Song of Songs,* the first publication of Elbert Hubbard's Roycroft Press in East Aurora, New York, he sent his order in "a low-comedy envelope done in watercolor."[44] An amused Hubbard asked if the artist might be willing to do some work for him. "People buy hand-painted china and pay a hundred dollars a piece, . . . will they do so for books? . . . There is no competition in this line, for the reason there is no demand. It is a virgin field. Now, having spied out the land, can you and I go in and possess it? Do you want to cast your lot and couple your name with Roycroft?"[45] Indeed Denslow did! "I have often wished that you would use illustrations in the *Philistine* as then I might hope to some day become a contributor," he replied.[46] Denslow saw by Hubbard's letters that "he was a great, strong man who could do me much good, and I did not have to be greatly urged to go to East Aurora with my paints and brushes, to give him the best in me."[47] He therefore became one of the first artists associated with the Roycroft Shops, and between 1896 and 1901, he spent a few months each year in East Aurora, doing all sorts of work for the firm. Then he turned around and used his earnings to buy the company's books, furniture, and other merchandise!

Elbert Hubbard, a former soap salesman and advertising man, was one of the first Americans to put William Morris and John Ruskin's progressive theories into action and set up a socialist community in East Aurora, just outside of Buffalo. The business—from fine book publication in imitation of Ruskin's Kelmscott Press to the manufacture of all kinds of other arts and crafts—swiftly grew beyond Hubbard's wildest expectations. An assortment of people drifted into this free society; those who suited Hubbard were given a place to live and work. And they were expected to work. Those who did not fit his needs were given the "four o'clock" (the next train out of town). Being the same age, Hubbard and Denslow got on splendidly. Calling himself "Fra Elbertus," Hubbard affectionately referred to the artist as "Deacon Denslow." (Hubbard may well have been the one who christened his friend "Hippocampus Den.") Denslow was also the "Growler," "a gruff, outspoken individual." Elbert Hubbard II recalled that "people didn't tamper with him much. He was one of the few men of his ilk—literary and artistic—who were here at different times that didn't in one way or another ever scrap with the 'boss.'"[48] Hubbard was also fond of Ann Waters Denslow, who accompanied her husband; her pretty face graced the frontispiece of Hubbard's *Time and Chance* (1899).

One of the Roycrofters Denslow did "scrap" with was an irrepressible handyman, Anson A. Blackman, whom Denslow nicknamed "Ali Baba of

Denslow's caricature of the Roycroft handyman, Anson Blackman, in the *Philistine,* August 1900

the Forty Thieves" and gave a quick kick in the pants for helping himself to the artist's tobacco jar. (Blackman later denied the charge and claimed he never smoked in his life! Nevertheless, no one touched Denslow's tobacco and got away with it.) Hubbard's son recalled the artist "working at his drawing board, smoking a corncob pipe, with a big bowl of tobacco on one side and another big bowl of burnt matches on the other. He'd get about two or three puffs out of a match and then have to relight. He smoked more matches than he did tobacco."[49] Blackman became famous as the frequent brunt of Hubbard's jokes and Denslow's cartoons, and the two conspired on a mock biography *So This Then Is the Appreciation of Ali Baba of East Aurora* (1899). Hubbard attributed many of the homespun aphorisms to the apparently illiterate and quite baffled Ali Baba. "Build your art horse-high, pig-tight, and bull-strong," he declared in one of Denslow's best cartoons.

The artist was not exempt from Hubbard's barbs. Once Denslow signed one of the Roycroft books wrong side up, and Hubbard added, "The fact that Den inscribed this book at the back and upside down is owing to another fact: i.e., the Roycrofters

Denslow at Roycroft with caricature of Anson Blackman, the Roycroft handyman, in the background, ca. 1899. Courtesy of Nancy Hubbard Brady

have recently opened a barrel of hard cider." Deacon Denslow gave as good as he got. Friendly caricatures of Fra Elbertus appeared in the *Philistine* from time to time. "Of more value to me than all else I have received for my work there," Denslow said of East Aurora, "is the good that has been done me because of being thrown against so strong and fine a character as is this same robust philosopher of East Aurora. His mind is strong; he is healthy, and he has the goods (gray matter) to deliver."[50]

Hubbard once said that his tombstone should read "He made them laugh and he made them mad—but he made them think." Considering himself an iconoclast, he filled his irreverent *Philistine* with all kinds of sardonic commentary. Denslow's sharp and sometimes caustic cartoons, attacking contemporary commerce, art, and religion, so fitted Hubbard's philosophy that they became a regular feature of the little journal. Stephen Crane, Andrew Carnegie, and the Muckrakers were all fair game for Denslow's barbed pen. He did gentler caricatures for the *Erudite,* another little magazine published by Hubbard's friend and first biographer Albert Lane. So aligned in temperament were

Cat. 24 John de Luxe [caricature of Elbert Hubbard], 1900 Courtesy of the New York Public Library, Astor, Lenox and Tilden Foundations

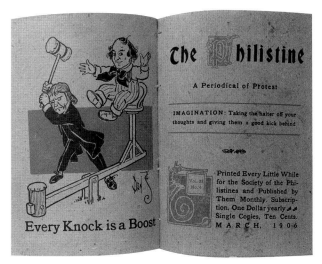

Cartoon for the *Philistine,* February 1906

Denslow and Hubbard, that Denslow redesigned the *Philistine* by adding his famous sea horse to the standard cover; it appeared in every issue from May 1899 until the magazine folded in July 1915 after Hubbard went down with the *Lusitania.*

The Roycrofters also distributed Denslow's most famous print, "What's the Use?" This scornful comment on the futility of life depicted a grinning, laurel-crowned skull comfortably posed on a copy of *Omar Khayyam.* Less popular but no less cynical was its antiwar companion "Victory," showing the same skull in a Roman helmet. One of the best of his *Philistine* cartoons, "Books to Burn," depicts a monk sitting on copies of the *Philistine,* another Roycroft title, and *The Book of Job* and poking a bonfire made up of other volumes. Denslow reworked the drawing as a poster advertising the entire Roycroft line. Denslow also helped design the Roycroft Library, and Hubbard had Denslow's drawings framed and hung about the shop. Perhaps the most remarkable of all his work for the Roycrofters was a set of Hippocampus andirons based on his well-known logo and issued in two sizes.

Denslow's sea horse worked its way into the watermark of the hand-made paper Hubbard imported from Europe for use in the books Denslow designed for the press. During his annual visits to East Aurora, Denslow produced a steady stream of covers, title pages, and sets of pseudomedieval ornamental initials that were used interchangeably from book to book, whether *Sonnets from the Portuguese* (1898), *Confessions of an Opium Eater* (1898), *The Deserted Village* (1898) or Hubbard's own best-seller *A Message to Garcia* (1899). A Denslow cover graced Hubbard's 1899 piracy of Rudyard Kipling's *Dipsy Chanty* until the poet successfully sued to have the publication suppressed for copyright infringement. Certainly the most elaborate of the Roycroft titles Denslow decorated was the so-called limited edition of Samuel Taylor Coleridge's *So This then Is ye Rime of the Ancient Mariner* (1899), followed by a more modest but still handsome embellishment of the Edward Fitzgerald translation of *The Rubaiyat of Omar Khayyam* (1899). Hubbard arranged for Denslow to design special bookplates for customers and turned to him to extra-illustrate copies of *Art and Life* (1896) by "Vernon Lee" (Violet Paget) and Hubbard's *As It Seems to Me* (1898) with highly finished watercolors, no two alike. Denslow also instructed the young women of East Aurora in how to hand-illuminate the books. Being just another member of the community, Denslow did not always sign his work, and Hubbard did not always credit him. Nevertheless, according to biographer Lane, to Denslow, "more than to any other man, excepting Mr. Hubbard, are due the individuality and originality that have made those East Aurora productions so charm-

ingly attractive. He is an artist of positive merit, brilliant in ideas, and wonderfully facile in the work of caricature."[51]

Hubbard was an eccentric publisher. He offered Roycroft books only by mail and often printed spurious information about the size of the press runs. Most books were not limited editions; Hubbard continuously reprinted them to meet the demand. Despite colophon information stating the press run was of 300 copies, there might be as many 1,500 in print. Also, the materials he used were not always of the high quality they were advertised to be. Not even Hubbard's signature was trustworthy; he relied on his staff to sign many of the books. While many contemporaries doubted Hubbard's sincerity, calling him nothing more than a vulgar huckster who exploited his workers, Denslow defended him as a person "of highest morals, earnest, a student and conscientious artist."[52] And Hubbard could not have been happier with his "Leonardo da Vinci of the North Side." He informed readers of the October 1896 issue of the *Philistine:* "Den draws things, paints divinely, is a good collar-and-elbow philosopher, an all-round wit, a storyteller of no mean repute, and . . . occasionally drops into poetry. . . . Happy Den! He doesn't have to think: like a hippocampus, he just absorbs."

Denslow, too, did not limit himself to limited editions. In Chicago he drew dozens of spot illustrations for Montgomery Ward catalogues between autumn 1897

Cat. 77 Roycroft andirons with seahorse motif, designed by Denslow, ca. 1896

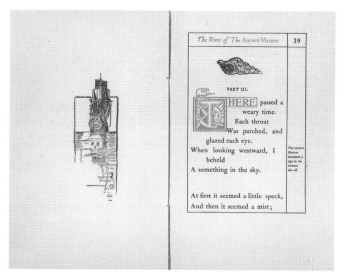

Cat. 74 Page design for *So This Then is ye Rime of ye Ancient Mariner,* 1899. Courtesy of the Chapin Library, Williams College

and winter 1900. He and Ann Waters contributed to *Carter's Monthly,* and he found time to do advertisements for Diamond Condensed Soups. When the Chicago Fine Arts Building opened in October 1898, Denslow joined commercial artists Ike Morgan, John T. McCutcheon, Will Carqueville, Frederick Richardson, Walter J. Enright, J. C. and Frank X. Leyendecker, Ralph Fletcher Seymour, Charles J. Costello, Fred W. Goudy, and Lawrence Mazzanovich in renting space. "Denslow's studio was a rendezvous for an interesting lot of newspapermen and artists," Seymour recalled. "At noon hours and after four o'clock afternoons several of them dropped in to talk, and for the first time I listened to the very keenest talk straight from newspaper row."[53] Denslow took every chance he could to promote the careers of the younger men, and he sat for a portrait by J. C. Leyendecker. Anyone in the arts was invited over to Denslow's studio for Ann Waters' delicious free lunches. One never knew who might drop by. Elbert Hubbard, George Ade, Otis Skinner, Will Crawford, Frank Pixley, and Harrison Fisher were just a few of the prominent visitors who signed the guest book.

It was through the Press Club that Denslow met Lyman Frank Baum, editor of the *Show Window,* a trade journal for window trimmers. Baum, through his work on the magazine, knew many of the artists at the Fine Arts Building, and he had already published a children's book *Mother Goose in Prose* (1897), the very first book illustrated by Maxfield Parrish. Something of a poet, Baum composed a collection of verse he called *By the Candelabra's Glare* (1898), set it in type, and printed it on a home press. He asked his artist friends for pictures, and Denslow supplied two for "My Quandary" and "The Greedy Goldfish." Denslow later drew a cover for the *Show Window* (December 1899), and when Baum decided to expand the slight selection of children's rhymes in *By the Candelabra's Glare* into a picture book, he readily turned to Denslow for the illustrations.

The two had little in common beside being the same age, but they did get on well at first. They often met at Baum's home in the evenings to go over their progress on the new children's book. The artist "had a striking red vest of which he was inordinately fond," one of Baum's sons remembered. "And whenever he came to our house, he would always complain of the heat as an excuse to take off his coat and spend the evening displaying his beautiful red vest. The family used to joke about it among ourselves, but it was a touchy subject with Denslow."[54] What most vividly impressed Baum's wife Maud was that the artist burned a hole in her best table cloth!

With the odors of Baum's cigar and Denslow's pipe filling the parlor, Baum read aloud his latest verses while Denslow sketched. Not only did Denslow illustrate the rhymes as soon as Baum composed them, but on occasion some drawing by Denslow suggested a verse to Baum. Soon they had ready a book for young readers that was unlike any then on the market. There were no immediate takers. Baum and Denslow knew that children preferred color images to black and whites, but this was an expensive novelty. The two men realized they would have to pay to get the book published just as they wanted it. Agreeing to share all expenses equally, they copyrighted it in both their names, and because their modern *Mother Goose's Melody* had a format similar to Palmer Cox's best-selling *The Brownies, Their Book* (1887), they settled on calling it *Father Goose, His Book.*

Denslow had just completed the cover of *The American Pure Food Cook Book and Household Economist* (1899) for George M. Hill Company, so he and Baum took the project to that large Chicago-based jobber to see if it might manufacture their children's book. Hill was so impressed with the dummy they presented that he offered to publish *Father Goose* on a royalty basis if Baum and Denslow paid to have all the colorplates made, including those for the covers, endpapers, and posters. The result was a revolutionary book that introduced Walter Crane's concept of "the art of the book" in a form that was designed for children. Every element, from cover to endpaper to title page to each page in the book, added to the entire design of the volume.

Baum and Denslow were determined to keep the printing costs down yet make their book as distinctive as possible. Denslow experimented with several color schemes before coming up with one of yellow, gray, orange, and black. He drew all the pictures in India ink with the flat two-dimensionality of Japanese art, and he provided some highlighting in red and a little dry brush for contrast. He and the printers worked on the color separations to make the pages as startling and bright as his posters, relying on the bold black outline and simple compositions of those earlier designs. Denslow had filled the pictures with his own wry humor to appeal to children and adults alike. In several of them he introduced a pictorial running gag that became a signature device in all his children's books: a chorus line of characters who varied only slightly from one another in dress or facial feature.

To further emphasize the decorative qualities of the pictures, Denslow and Baum hired Ralph Fletcher Seymour to hand-letter the text, which also saved them the cost of having the verses set in type. Seymour was at first skeptical about the terms, but they offered the very last page of the book to serve as both an acknowledgement of his contribution to *Father Goose* and an advertisement for his work. Unable to do all of it himself, Seymour then hired Charles J. Costello to help him, and they fully captured the spirit of Denslow's drawing in their capable lettering. The final result was a children's book that looked like a collection of art posters.

Having risked their own money, Baum and Denslow aggressively sent complimentary copies of *Father Goose* to anyone they could think of, everyone from author William Dean Howells to Admiral Dewey. "I read *Father Goose* through for my own amusement," Elbert Hubbard informed them; "then I read it to the Roycroft baby; then the Roycroft baby read it to me—at least, explained all the pictures, one by one. And now each night for a week the baby has brought me the book and I've had to read it through to her. If there is any higher praise can be given a book than it interests grown-ups and fascinates the babies, why I do not know it. In the Roycroft Shop *Father Goose* has caused two chuckles to grow where there was only one before."[55] Ann Waters sent a copy to Mark Twain, an old family friend. Thanking its creators "in the name of the child world for making it," the author of *Tom Sawyer* and *Huckleberry Finn* declared that

Father Goose marked the beginning of a new era in juvenile literature. Twain assured them, *"Father Goose* has a double chance of succeeding: parents will buy him ostensibly for the nursery so that they may privately smuggle him out and enjoy him themselves."[56]

The novelty of the book garnered all kinds of free publicity, some of it at Denslow's personal instigation and for his personal profit. He included drawings for *Father Goose* in a large commercial art show at the Fine Arts Building and put others on display in several department store windows in Chicago and elsewhere. When the New York *World* devoted a full page to the book, Paul West, editor of the Sunday comic supplement, queried Denslow: "If I should send you a good idea, and, on your working it up for a page, gave you full credit as author of

Cat. 66 Poster, *Father Goose, His Book,* ca. 1899

Father Goose's picture, wouldn't you be willing to do the drawing 'very reasonable' for us?"[57] Denslow was willing. He did two pages for the *World,* "Father Goose Shows the Children How to Run a Double-Runner—The Awful Result" (January 21, 1900) and "Father Goose at the Seashore" (July 22, 1900), the latter with verses by West. Neither page mentioned Baum.

Baum wrote in the introduction that *Father Goose* contained "newer jingles and pictures for children of today" that were "intended solely to supplement the nursery rhymes of our ancestors." He and Denslow had invigorated the old sedate form by infusing it with the energy of urban American life. *Father Goose* was one of the few children's books that did not recognize the United States as all white. However insensitive some of the verses

Cat. 6 Dust jacket design for *Father Goose, His Book,* 1899.

and pictures may be by today's standards, they celebrated a multicultural city. The book was bold, brash, and in places vulgar, but not dull. It was sophisticated, but hardly refined. In *Father Goose,* art nouveau encountered contemporary American slapstick. Like Chicago itself, there was nothing pretty or precious about *Father Goose.* Even today, almost a century later, many of the pictures remain remarkably fresh and inventive.

Success breeds imitation. Immediately a horde of *Father Goose*-like books flocked to the bookstores—*Old Father Gander* (1899), *Baby Goose, His Adventures* (1900), *Mr Bunny, His Book* (1900), *Daddy Long Legs* (1900), *Kids of Many Colors* (1900), and others—most by friends of Baum and Denslow's. Even they were quick to capitalize on their best seller by issuing *The Songs of Father Goose* (1900), a selection of the verse and pictures with music by Alberta N. Hall. For this title and a quartet of song folios taken from the book that Hill published the same year, Denslow designed new covers and title pages.[58]

In 1900 Baum and Denslow were America's most important new children's book team. While their first book was at press they were hard at work on their next project. They knew that the new one, "a modernized fairy tale" as Baum called it, was an even bigger risk. They had such little faith in the work that their letter of agreement contained an odd clause stating that if fewer than 10,000 copies sold within two years, "this contract may be declared null and void by either Baum or Denslow, in which case said Baum shall be declared

sole owner of the text and said Denslow sole owner of the illustrations, to be used independently each of the other."[59] What Denslow might have done with a whole set of pictures without any story is anyone's guess, but they need not have worried. Hill readily gave them an advance of $1,000 against royalties on a children's book tentatively called "The City of Oz," but he offered much the same terms as before: Baum and Denslow were to be entirely responsible for the costs of making the color plates. As in the case of *Father Goose,* Baum and Denslow registered the copyright of the book in both their names.

Denslow's more than 100 two-color text illustrations and 24 full-color plates made *The Wonderful Wizard of Oz* the most lavishly produced children's books of its day. (The average contemporary juvenile book contained no more than a dozen black-and-white pictures.) As he had with *Father Goose,* Denslow adhered to the principles of "the art of the book" to produce the most complex and highly sophisticated example of decorative art. To introduce more novelty into the story and its embellishment, Baum had his tale embrace a rainbow of colors as it passed from one locale to another. Gray Kansas gave way to the blue land of the Munchkins which was followed by the red Deadly Poppy Field, the green Emerald City, the yellow country of the Winkies, the brown lands between the capital of Oz and the red Quadling Country ruled by Glinda the Good Witch. Denslow's textual designs included spot illustrations, chapter-title pages, head- and tailpieces, and double-page spreads. The last were among the first pic-

Portrait of L. Frank Baum, 1899.
Courtesy of the late Joslyn Stanton Baum

tures in any children's book to bleed to the edges of the pages.

The full-page pictures Denslow restricted to 24 color plates. Although he drew them only in India ink, no black appears in the printed images. The key block was instead a deep blue, the other three colors were yellow, red, and pale blue. These colors produced some startling results, particularly Dorothy's bright yellow face. Because he expected to direct the printers in what they should do, Denslow took certain shortcuts in his drawing. He indicated large spaces of flat color without actually filling them all in, and he often designated reverse lettering with black line, all because he knew that printers could easily do what was required on the specific plates. Because he was away for part of the winter, Denslow may not have seen the final proofs of his pictures; a number of his directions were not carried out and had to be corrected in the second printing of the book.

The illustrator's considerable contribution to the success of *The Wizard of Oz* should not be underestimated. Lewis Carroll had his John Tenniel, and Baum had his Denslow, and this project certainly brought out the best in the artist. Denslow never again did anything quite so remarkable as these pictures. This quintessential American fairy tale gave him

Denslow at his drawing board, ca. 1899
Private collection

the opportunity to design an entire secondary world that entered the country's folklore. Denslow admitted that a fantasy such as Baum's demanded that he "work out and invent characters, costumes, and a multitude of other details for which there is no data— and there never can be in original fairy stories."[60] He had to devise an unique style of architecture for the land of Oz. Domed Munchkin houses smile at visitors; the magnificent City of Emeralds is built out of elements from the Near Eastern architecture of *A Cruise under the Crescent* and from the opulent but temporal beaux arts buildings of the 1893 World's Columbian Exposition. Here too may be found faces staring out of the jewel-encrusted architecture.

Baum populated his fairy tale with an extraordinary cast of characters that tested Denslow's powers of invention at every turn in the Road of Yellow Bricks. He took special pains in depicting Scarecrow and Tin Woodman. "I made twenty-five sketches of those two monkeys before I was satisfied with them," he recalled. "I experimented with all sorts of straw waistcoats and sheet-iron cravats before I was satisfied."[61] He transformed the Cowardly Lion into an exceptional example of comic characterization worthy of comparison with A. B. Frost's Br'er Rabbit and E. H. Shepard's Toad of Toad Hall. Denslow pro-

Cat. 5 *Father Goose, His Book*, 1899. Courtesy of the New York Public Library, Astor, Lenox and Tilden Foundations

Cat. 18
Titlepage for *The Wonderful Wizard of Oz*, 1900

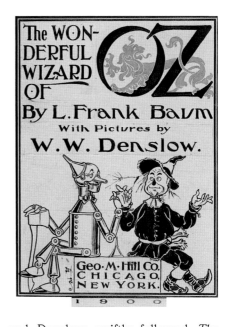

vided Munchkins, Winkies, and Quadlings with distinctive national costumes, and Kalidahs, Winged Monkeys, Fighting Trees, and Hammerheads all came to life through his pen. The only major criticism Denslow received for his pictures was for his failure to draw Dorothy as a childlike child. But few readers seemed to mind. *The Wizard of Oz* with its compelling fairy tale and extraordinary pictures succeeded *Father Goose* as the best-selling children's book of the year. It had everything—magic, adventure, danger, humor, and some of the most inventive illustrations of any juvenile in years.

Cat. 21 Cover illustration for *The Songs of Father Goose*, 1900

Baum and Denslow swiftly followed *The Wizard of Oz* with *Dot and Tot of Merryland* (1901), another modern fairy tale. Baum proudly wrote in the preface "Mr. Denslow's quaint and merry pictures . . . in this book excel all his previous work." Certainly Denslow's drawings are prettier than his previous work, and the little heroine looks more childlike, but the storyline is less exciting an adventure. By sending two little children on the exploration of the seven valleys of Merryland, Baum did supply the artist with all sorts of delightful secondary characters—dolls, toy soldiers, clowns, kittens, babies, candy people, and mechanical toys—to dance and skip and jump and race across the pages. Denslow made up for the absence of colorplates by creating a riot of textual illustrations handsomely printed in black, cocoa brown, and vermillion. These were even more decorative than in the two men's previous collaborations and are sometimes as finely executed as anything the English illustrator Charles Robinson was then doing in his children's books. Denslow's designs are more marginalia that embellish than true illustrations that carry the story along, and without any landscapes or detailed interiors to speak of, the pictures offer no real sense of

34

place. Unlike Oz, one does not know exactly what Merryland looks like. It is all a pleasant and pretty diversion in which not much happens in either story or pictures. Sales were disappointing.

It was growing clear to Denslow in 1901 that he must prove that he no longer needed Baum. The two had already clashed over which of them was more responsible for the success of their books. Baum was publishing other books with other illustrators, and he did not have to share royalty or copyright with them. Denslow's principal work for that year was not *Dot and Tot of Merryland* but a far more ambitious volume: *Denslow's Mother Goose*, a safely conservative choice produced for McClure, Phillips and Company, New York, an energetic young firm founded by S. S. McClure of the muckraking *McClure's Magazine.* Determined to make a name for itself in the juvenile market, the publisher was as eager as Denslow to make the book a resounding success. "You bet the *Mother Goose* will be a winner," the artist confidently wrote old friend Charles Waldron in October. "We are not able to fill all orders yet, but will soon. The workmanship on this book I don't think can be beaten. No money has been spared to make it take its place at the top of the heap. We don't acknowledge any competition. As for my part of it, why, I think I have made a reasonable improvement. As for the rhymes, I have just taken the old stuff of our childhood."[62] Indeed the publisher did not stint on production; this big, handsome book remains one of the best and brightest editions of *Mother Goose* ever published in the United States. It is also one of the least appreciated.

Denslow's Mother Goose was the first fully contemporary interpretation of the old rhymes, and it contains none of the nostalgia for preindustrial eighteenth-century England of Walter Crane's, Kate Greenaway's, or Randolph Caldecott's pictures. (The handsome twentieth-century editions illustrated by L. Leslie Brooke, Jessie Willcox Smith, Ethel Franklin Betts, Blanche Fisher Wright, Frederick Richardson, Marguerite di Angeli, and Tasha Tudor all belong to that Victorian tradition.) Denslow produced a modern *Mother Goose* for modern boys and girls. This was not just any old *Mother Goose;* this was Denslow's *Mother Goose.* "The object of this book primarily is to furnish fun for the children," he explained. "I have taken the liberty of editing the old, original text slightly and in doing so have attempted to retain the bright verses, replete with action, expression and wholesome fun, eliminating those so justly condemned by careful mothers and teachers of the present day."[63]

Arguing, as did Baum, that children's books should be free of all unpleasant details, Denslow saw no reason to "always adhere strictly to the text of all the familiar nursery rhymes. I believe in pure fun for the children, and I believe it can be given them without any incidental gruesomeness. In my *Mother Goose* I did not hesitate to change the text where the

Cat. 19 Cover design for *The Wonderful Wizard of Oz,* 1900

35

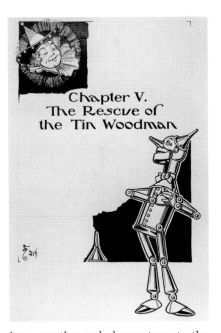

change would give a gentler and clearer tone to the verse. The comic element isn't lost in this way."[64] Actually he kept major changes to a minimum. His old woman who lived in a shoe "kissed them all fondly" rather than "beat them all soundly." The father who goes a-hunting will "never get this rabbit's skin / To wrap the baby bunting in!" In general Denslow turned to the best known and least controversial rhymes and merely modernized their context. For example, he portrayed Little Arthur in "Rain, rain, go away" as a golfer and put a "To Let" sign on the home of the man in the moon when he came down too soon. Denslow's was also an American *Mother Goose.* "Papa" became "Daddy"; waiters brought ice water to the woman who lived on nothing but victuals and drink; and the child in "Hush-a-bye, baby, on the tree top" was a little American Indian on his cradle board. Denslow also christened the vessel of the wise men of Gotham "The Bowl of N. Y.," thus connecting two names for that great American city. He provided other clever new interpretations of the old rhymes. He indicated how the Man in the Moon could burn his mouth on "cold pease porridge" by placing Tabasco and other spices on the table; he may have been the first to depict

Jack-be-nimble as a jolly dog jumping over the candlestick.

The book was tailor-made for young children. Denslow had simplified his forms and compositions even more than before and minimized most of the double-page spreads to bright white pages facing those with a flat marine green that bled to the margins. The illustrations are almost emblematic with no unnecessary detail or gratuitous gesture to distract bright little eyes. The figures are also larger than in his previous children's book pictures, the humor as broad and obvious as possible to induce young laughter. His limited color scheme relied on the unique but unexpectedly soothing interplay of orange, peach, marine green, and black.

As with *Father Goose,* Denslow gave all the pages of *Mother Goose* a poster quality by having the rhymes hand-lettered, this time by Fred W. Goudy, (later one of the country's most distinguished type-designers). Goudy recalled that Denslow "had lettered the title page and one or two of the jingles, when he realized that as a letterer he was a much better illustrator. He came to me and said I would letter one or two pages for him and he could then decide whether he wished me to do the work. I did the 'Humpty-Dumpty sat on a wall' page, which pleased him. After looking over the copy, I found a number of the rhymes required only four to six lines for the work, a few longer, and I named a price of two dollars each page for the work. He was amazed—he had expected to pay much more for the lettering. Another thing he liked was the rapidity with which I turned it out (I needed the money)." The resulting "face" expertly conformed to the quality of Denslow's line. "To do the lettering expeditiously," Goudy explained, "I developed a form of letter at once distinctive and, for me, easy to execute more or less rapidly. The ascenders and descenders were short, the height of the short letters like a, o, c, e, m, n, etc., was noticeably high in relation to the ascenders and descendants." (To Goudy's dismay, Inland Type Foundry of St. Louis took the lettering "without bothering to acquire rights of reproduction, made it into type, and—horror of horrors—named it 'Hearst'!") Denslow rewarded Goudy for his vital contribution by giving him the final page of the book to serve as both a credit line and an advertisement for his wares. The book's printer proudly reported to Goudy "that often his six-or-seven-year-old son sat on his lap evenings and the boy would go over every page of the *Mother Goose,* reading the jingles aloud, and when he came to the colophon: 'The verses in this book have been hand-lettered by Fred. W. Goudy,' he would read that too, as one of the Mother Goose Rhymes."[65]

This modern *Mother Goose* was one of the best-selling juveniles of the year. "Denslow's new book will give undiluted joy to anyone between the ages of two and one hundred," announced writer George Ade. "It is the most satisfying children's book that I've seen."[66] Declaring his independence of Baum, Denslow had made a success with his very first try. But despite good reviews and strong sales, not every one cared for his books. How could anything so popular be any good? A backlash against his work was already growing among the country's librarians. Caroline M. Hewins of the Hartford Public Library

Cat. 11 Chapter VI. The Cowardly Lion, 1900. Courtesy of the New York Public Library, Astor, Lenox and Tilden Foundations

had called Baum and Denslow's *Father Goose* "silly and sometimes coarse."[67] But perhaps the most damaging criticism came from Anne Carroll Moore, children's librarian at Pratt Institute Free Library in Brooklyn (later the country's most powerful children's librarian as head of Work with Children at the New York Public Library). "Most of the popular picture books of the time are unworthy of a place in the hands of children," she warned. "Such books as *Denslow's Mother Goose* and Baum's *Father Goose,* with a score of others of the comic poster order, should be banished from the sight of impressionable little children."[68] Neither Hewins nor Moore ever explained exactly what she objected to in Denslow's illustrations, but both preferred the more refined, more genteel picture books of English artists Crane, Greenaway, and Caldecott and of French designer Louis-Maurice Boutet de Monvel to anything by any contemporary American.

"To make children laugh," Denslow countered, "you must tell them stories of action. They aren't really fascinated by cruelty—it's action they want. The trouble is that their desires have been misunderstood. I tell my stories with pictures, and I can often indicate action by expression. Action and expression, then, are two of my mainstays, and when you had the incongruous, you have the triad that I rely on."[69] The many letters Denslow received from parents all over the country, made it obvious that the children liked his

pictures even if some librarians did not. "From the
kids you can always get unbiased criticism," he
believed. "They don't play favorites, and there is no
way you can tamper with the witnesses. They like a
thing, or they don't. And if they like it, they demand
more of it." He added, "It has been my experience
that when you can reach the youngsters you can
reach their elders also."[70]

The resounding success of *Denslow's Mother
Goose* and relative failure of *Dot and Tot of Merryland*
proved to Denslow that he did not need Baum or any
collaborator to prosper in the juvenile book field. *Dot
and Tot of Merryland* was Baum and Denslow's last
book together.[71] However much they may have
enjoyed doing *Father Goose, Wizard of Oz,* and *Dot
and Tot of Merryland,* they were never close friends.
Theirs was primarily a business relationship. The bank-
ruptcy of George M. Hill in early 1902, provided them
with a convenient reason to part company.

Disputes over a musical extravaganza based on
The Wizard of Oz gave them an even stronger excuse.
In 1901 young concert pianist and composer Paul
Tietjens, a friend of Denslow's, had proposed to Baum
that they turn the children's story into an operetta.
Baum initially agreed only if Denslow were not
involved; however, once Baum and Tietjens had failed
to place their first musical collaboration with a producer, Denslow was brought in and the three men
began negotiating in earnest on a staging of *The
Wizard of Oz.* After months of squabbling, the ama-
teurs finally signed a contract on September 21, 1901,
which stipulated that Denslow "will design the costumes for the characters in the said libretto, and the
illustrations for posters and other advertising paper of
the production" and that "Denslow shall also be adver-

tised in the paper of the production, in the usual cus-
tomary manner, as the designer of the costumes and
the advertising posters and any other artistic work that
he may perform for the benefit and promotion of the
said production." It was also Denslow's responsibility
to represent the three of them "in securing a proper
presentation of said operatic production and shall
transact all business details connected with such presentation for the mutual benefit of all concerned in this
contract."[72] (Nine days later, apparently without
Denslow's knowledge, Baum and Tietjens copyrighted
the musical composition of *The Wonderful Wizard
of Oz* in their names only.) Denslow mentioned the
project to his good friend William T. "Biff" Hall, drama
critic with the Chicago *Tribune* and New York
Dramatic Mirror, and Hall introduced Denslow to Fred
A. Hamlin, who finally produced the show at
Chicago's Grand Opera House. The musical opened
on June 16, 1902, to rave reviews, especially for Fred
Stone and David Montgomery in the roles of the

Scarecrow and Tin Woodman. It went on the road and landed on Broadway in early 1903, making fortunes for all concerned.

In the end, Denslow was almost completely cut out of the musical's actual preparation. Someone else was brought in to provide the bulk of the costumes, and Denslow never designed any posters or other advertising for the show. The only credit he received was a minor one in the program: "Character Costumes by W. W. Denslow (the illustrator of the book)." And Tietjens later claimed that Denslow could not have done any more than six.[73] Denslow was so uninvolved with the production that he did not see it until the first week in August, nearly six weeks after it opened. Although Baum's original libretto and much of Tietjens's score were also scrapped long before *The Wizard of Oz* reached the stage, they always resented that Denslow profited just as handsomely as they did during the show's long, successful run.

The tension between Denslow and Baum was in part acerbated by Denslow's poor health. Although there is nothing in the pictures to suggest it, strain from working on *Dot and Tot of Merryland* and

Cat. 12
Chapter VIII. The Deadly Poppy Field, 1900. Courtesy of the New York Public Library, Astor, Lenox and Tilden Foundations

Denslow's Mother Goose finally led to physical collapse in April 1901, and Denslow sought treatment for "nervous prostrate" and rheumatism at Alma Sanitarium in Alma, Michigan, where he continued to work despite severe pain that forced him to rely on a stenographer for his correspondence. The artist became great friends with the sanitarium's director Dr. George F. Butler, for whom Denslow designed a letterhead and the cover for his health journal the *Doctor's Magazine; or, How to Live.* He also met and fell in love with Frances Golsen Doolittle, who was a wealthy widow even younger than Ann Waters and who had a six-year-old daughter also named Frances. When he returned to Chicago in May, Denslow informed Ike Morgan that "it was impossible for him to live with his wife any longer"; soon after he and Ann Waters separated. "Mr. Denslow refused to live with me as his wife," she recalled. "He said he no longer loved me."[74] Yet whatever their differences may have been, Denslow did dedicate his *Mother Goose* to her "with much love and gratitude for her help in its making." (The two briefly reconciled; she accompanied him on his move to New York City later that year and on his first trip to Bermuda that winter but then returned to Chicago.)

With his marriage shaky and his partnership with Baum dissolved, there was nothing to keep Denslow in Chicago. He had never cared much for the city, referring to it as "one immense cash register."[75] Despite his success there, the control that the Chicago publishing, engraving, and printing companies wielded over artists left him disgruntled. "The businessman is the great man; he is the whole thing, and he shows it clearly and distinctly. The artist or writer, what is he? He is my hired man, my money buys him, to me belongs the credit. The arms of Chicago should be . . . a sluggish sewer with two branches, a Hog Rampant on a field of orr, supported by two shorn lambs. Crest: a setting Hen on a gold brick. Motto: ah there! get there!"[76] Denslow knew he could do better; back East provided far more possibilities for a successful illustrator to further prosper.

In New York, Denslow quickly entered the highly lucrative comic strip industry. Since that day back in 1895 when Richard F. Outcault scrawled some odd comments on the yellow night shirt of a big-eared, gap-toothed guttersnipe and created the Yellow Kid, the first sustained Sunday-comic character, the funnies had grown into an enormously profitable business. A number of prominent children's book illustrators, including Peter Newell, E. W. Kemble, Palmer Cox, and Harrison Cady eventually broke into the business, but Denslow was one of the very first. The newly formed newspaper syndicate S. S. McClure Co. (actually founded by T. C. McClure, brother of the publisher of *Denslow's Mother Goose*) was eager to cut into the funny paper market and was happy to hire such a widely known artist as Denslow to create a series for the first issue of its new color Sunday supplement.

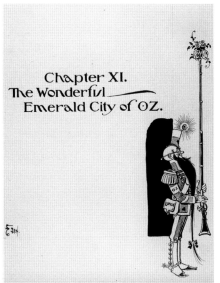

On November 11, 1901, Denslow introduced his weekly fairy tale in pictures called "Billy Bounce." Its story line was simple but highly flexible: the amusing adventures of a little messenger boy who wears an inflatable suit that like a great rubber ball allows him to bounce from one episode to the next. Denslow effortlessly adapted his picture-book style to the new form, so the brilliantly colored and well-designed "Billy Bounce" quickly became one of the most artistically attractive of all the early comic strips (which in those days took up full pages). The broad humor, strong outline, simple shapes, and absence of secondary detail made Denslow's drawings perfectly suited to funny page illustration. Denslow obviously enjoyed playing with the form and extended its possibilities while generally avoiding the coarseness so characteristic of contemporary Sunday funnies such as "The Katzenjammer Kids," "Foxy Grampa," and "Happy Hooligan." Denslow insisted that his strip would provide a more genteel comic page for young readers, one free of the cruel pranks and other slapstick that children thought hilarious and parents found offensive. Other cartoonists recognized his innovations and put them to good use in their strips.

Having a syndicated weekly comic page that appeared in papers all over the country gave Denslow's work greater visibility than it had ever had before, and just in time for Christmas, he shrewdly introduced some characters from *Denslow's Mother Goose* into "Billy Bounce" to help promote the new book. Denslow drew other strips, notably "Strenuous Bobby" in 1902, but none of them often caught on like "Billy Bounce." There were "Billy Bounce" cigars, "Billy Bounce" penny banks, "Billy Bounce" buttons, a "Billy Bounce" march. At least one child was named

Cat. 22 Color sketch for *Denslow's Mother Goose,* 1901. Courtesy of the New York Public Library, Astor, Lenox and Tilden Foundations

after the popular character. But by August 3, 1902, Denslow had tired of drawing the strip week after week; McClure turned it over to Charles W. Kahles, who successfully continued it for several more years. (Kahles went on to draw "Sandy Highflyer" and "Hairbreadth Harry," which have been erroneously termed the first "story-strips.")

While diligently drawing the weekly "Billy Bounce" episode, the artist did not neglect his children's books. *Denslow's Night Before Christmas* appeared in 1902, perhaps suggested by Baum's latest fairy tale, *The Life and Adventures of Santa Claus* (1902). Denslow's interpretation of Clement C. Moore's famous poem "A Visit from St. Nicholas" is one of the liveliest ever published, as jolly as Old St. Nick himself. Like everyone else in

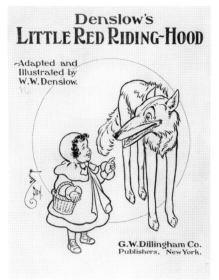

Cat. 30 Cover for *Denslow's Little Red Riding Hood,* 1903

America, Denslow knew Thomas Nast's famous conception of this patron saint of childhood and may have based some of his pictures on Nast's cartoons in *Harper's Weekly* and *Young People,* but he transformed that "right jolly old elf" into an urbane and remarkably nimble Santa garbed in an elegant green fur suit.

There was nothing traditional about *Denslow's Night Before Christmas.* His compositions were heavily Japanese in spirit. One especially fine touch was contrasting the snoozing living room prior to Santa's arrival with the subsequent picture of it enlivened with presents. This time Denslow hand-lettered the text himself. And he devised a color scheme in which a preponderant peacock blue was paired with vermillion, pumpkin yellow, olive, and black. He filled the pages with an assortment of wonderful toys and happy tots and as usual indulged in a little self-advertising by slipping a stuffed goose from *Denslow's Mother Goose* and a toy Tin Woodman into Santa's bag. (Before the book went on press he dropped a reference to *Father Goose* from the endpapers.) Denslow took the project to the G. W. Dillingham Company, a well-established New York firm that had never done much with children's books. *Denslow's Night Before Christmas* proved to be another enormous success; reportedly 30,000 copies were sold before publication.

Dillingham then issued "Denslow's Picture Books for Children," an ambitious eighteen volumes that in 1903 and 1904 appeared as individual pamphlets in two editions, one regular paper and another mounted on linen, and as three hardcover anthologies, *Denslow's Humpty Dumpty and Other Stories,* which included *Humpty Dumpty; Little Red Riding Hood; The Three Bears; Mary Had a Little Lamb; Old Mother Hubbard;* and *House That Jack Built,* (1903); *Denslow's One Ring Circus and Other Stories,* which included *One Ring Circus; Zoo; 5 Little Pigs; Tom Thumb; A B C Book;* and *Jack and the Bean-Stalk* (1903); and *Denslow's Scarecrow* and the *Tin-Man and Other Stories,* which included *Scarecrow* and the *Tin-Man; Barnyard Circus; Animal Fair; Mother Goose A B C Book; Simple Simon;* and *Three Little Kittens* (1904).[77] Contracted in September 1902, the new series actually made its debut as the delightful quartet "Denslow's Christmas Tales" in the New York *Herald's* special Christmas Edition (December 14, 1902) of its Sunday comic supplement. These bright, full-color pages were retellings of "Little Red

Riding Hood," "Humpty Dumpty Junior," "The Three Bears," and "Jack and the Bean-Stalk" in harmless but competent couplets, that Denslow then rendered in prose as part of his picture books.

Denslow's series constituted the first successful attempt by an American to emulate the famous British toybooks Crane and Caldecott produced with London printer Edmund Evans. Denslow drew on many of the same subjects but generally restricted his titles to juvenile lore only. These popular old nursery rhymes and tales were also the common property of the cheap picture books that had been published for years by the McLoughlin Brothers of New York and other large publishers of popular juvenile literature. F. O. C. Darley, Henry Louis Stephens, and Thomas Nast too had designed exceptional toybooks for the United States market, but Denslow's brassy pamphlets were the first to be thoroughly American and up-to-date in content and style. He confidently applied the vitality of the *fin-de-siècle* art poster and comic strip to the high aesthetic principles of the English arts and crafts movement. In the tradition of Crane's and Caldecott's toybooks, Denslow's covers, copyright and dedication notices, and every other page in the individual titles contributed to the total design of the series.

Cat. 69 Poster for *Denslow's Night Before Christmas,* 1902

But Denslow differed from his predecessors in his purpose for the books. Crane tried to elevate the taste of children; Denslow catered to their capabilities. Crane employed an expansive method; Denslow a reductive one. Denslow concentrated on the immediate subject at hand as he skillfully played with large geometric shapes and flat unpatterned masses of color against strong simple drawing that was free of any unnecessary diverting detail. Greenaway's and Boutet de Monvel's books were *about* children; Denslow's were *for* children. Denslow's aim was to entertain readers, and he achieved that by adapting his art to their level. As further proof of his commitment to the little ones, Denslow dedicated each title to the child of a friend; for example, he addressed *Denslow's Little Red Riding Hood* to actor Otis Skinner's infant daughter Cornelia, later a famous actress herself.

As in the past, there was nothing dainty or delicate about Denslow's designs. His energetic figures were always up to something, dancing, running, jumping, continually acting and reacting. They are little actors performing on a shallow stage. Aware of how much children love animals, Denslow filled his picture books with all sorts of amusing birds and beasts. By giving every one of them something different to do, Denslow provided prototypes for the self-absorbed little creatures of Richard Scarry's popular modern picture books. They are right out of the funny papers and animated cartoons with no apparent resemblance to any in nature. They belong to the zoo and circus rather than to the jungle and forest, and are having far too much fun imitating human beings to listen to the call of the wild. In Denslow's world of the Merry Mountains in Glad Lands, it is all smiles and laughter. The expressions he gave them derived from a long, careful study of comparative physiognomy, the gestures from a thorough knowledge of comparative anatomy. Their features reflect joy, fear, surprise, and every other human emotion. "The bear's face is by long odds the most adaptable to my purposes," Denslow admitted.[78] And he used any opportunity he could find to include one in a picture, even prominently in the poster for the 1904 volumes. Here and there in these books is some careless, clumsy drawing, no doubt due to the volume of work he had to do in such a short time, but the humor is as cheerily infectious as ever and ideal for preschoolers. Denslow did add little bits of sly comedy in his pictures that likely were lost on most youngsters. Particularly amusing is his caricature of L. Frank Baum as the cop in *Denslow's 5 Little Pigs.*

In the new series, the designer returned to the color scheme of *Denslow's Night Before Christmas,* a bright and brilliant contrast to the subdued palettes in the toybooks of Crane, Greenaway, and Caldecott. As before he expertly used the white of the page as another color in his designs. But this time Denslow chose a soft eggshell-colored paper that gave a soothing finish to the colors.

Again Denslow edited the text as he saw fit. He was hardly the first to rework the material, for the battle over the classic unexpurgated fairy tale as proper reading for the young had been raging for years. American author Samuel Griswold Goodrich wrote the first of his many popular "Peter Parley" books as an answer to all the rampant barbarism he found in traditional nursery lore. Then Charles Dickens accused George Cruikshank of "fraud on the fairies" for daring to rewrite such children's classics as "Jack and the Bean-Stalk" and "Cinderella" as temperance tracts in his "Fairy Library" of 1854. Denslow's attitude to the old stories and rhymes had a little bit of both Peter Parley and George Cruikshank about it. He thought the original "Jack and the Bean-Stalk" particularly offensive. "A lad gains admittance to a man's house under false pretenses," he recounted the English folk tale, "imposing on the sympathies of the man's wife. Then he commits theft after theft. . . . When the man attempts to defend his property he is slain by the hero, who mutilates the corpse to the extreme gratification of his mother. All childhood classics are not such glaring instances of rapine and murder, but they nearly all have a tendency in that direction, and I am trying to give the kids books that are more healthy in tone." In *Denslow's Jack and the Bean-Stalk,* the boy reforms the big bully and then with his mother grows rich by exhibiting the giant as a side-show freak. The grandmother in *Denslow's Little Red Riding Hood* beats the wolf so soundly that it agrees to becom-

Cat. 25 Titlepage for *Denslow's Night Before Christmas,* 1902. Courtesy of William Wagner

ing the very first watchdog. Likewise the bears in *Denslow's The Three Bears* are now tame and forgiving. And the artist kept King Arthur's tiny knight from being slain by a spider in *Denslow's Tom Thumb;* likewise he spared the egg in *Denslow's Humpty Dumpty* by hard boiling it! Denslow obviously felt he had no more reason to apologize for what he had done any more than had Cruikshank, saying, "When I illustrate and edit childhood classics I do not hesitate to expurgate."[79]

He found some long forgotten rhymes for *Denslow's Simple Simon,* included Sarah Josepha Hale's complete "Mary's Lamb" (1830) in *Denslow's Mary Had a Little Lamb,* and altered Sarah Catherine Martin's *The Comic Adventures of Old Mother Hubbard* (1805) to eliminate mentions of the dog's dying, coffins, or trips to the alehouse for some beer and the tavern for white wine and red. The monkey does not get drunk in *Denslow's Animal Fair,* instead the ex-drunkard offers such temperance beverages as tea, lemonade, and ginger ale. Several of the stories and verses Denslow entirely wrote himself. But while the pictures as always are fine, the prose in *Denslow's Barnyard Circus, Denslow's A B C Book, Denslow's Mother Goose A B C,* and the two stories of Peter Funnybones' adventures in Glad Lands—*Denslow's One Ring Circus* and *Denslow's Zoo*—lack literary distinction. Possibly with R. M. Ballantyne's picture book *The Three Little Kittens* (1856) partly in mind, he expanded on the famous verses attributed to Eliza Follen in *Denslow's Three Little Kittens.* For

Denslow's Humpty Dumpty, he wove an original fairy tale around the old nursery rhyme just as Baum had done in *Mother Goose in Prose.* "I don't think I make anything namby-pamby," he tried to defend himself, "nor do I eliminate the funny element in this work. I do not hesitate to say that where I illustrate and edit the childhood classics they will be expurgated editions and the children will not suffer from it one bit."[80] Change is not necessarily improvement. In stripping the old stories of their original intensity, he may indeed have been freeing them of their traditional coarseness, cruelty, and bloodshed, but he also cleansed them of their natural vigor and drama.

Certainly the most important of his picture books for 1904 was *Denslow's Scarecrow and the Tin-Man,* the artist's obvious attempt to reinforce his claim to *The Wonderful Wizard of Oz.* To capitalize on the fame of the musical extravaganza, L. Frank Baum and his new publishers Reilly and Britton, formerly with George M. Hill Company, announced for the autumn 1904 publication of a sequel to *The Wizard of Oz* tentatively called "The Further Adventures of the Scarecrow and the Tin Woodman" (later changed to *The Marvelous Land of Oz*). The pictures were provided by young Philadelphia newspaper artist John R. Neill. Denslow was neither consulted nor even considered for the job.

As co-owner of the copyright of *The Wizard of Oz,* Denslow thought he was completely justified in issuing his own Scarecrow and Tin Man book the same season as Baum's. (He had already used the two characters to represent "S is the Scarecrow" and "T is the Tin Man" in *Denslow's A B C Book.*) His was not a sequel to Baum's fairy tale but an original story about a musical-comedy team who run away from the theater and get into a series of mishaps before returning just in time for the evening performance. It was not much, but it did remind the public that Denslow was one of the creators of the popular play and the book on which it was based. Perhaps aware that Baum dedicated *The Marvelous Land of Oz* to Montgomery and Stone (stars of the musical extravaganza), Denslow appropriately

His eyes, how they twinkled! his

dimples how merry!

His cheeks were like roses, his

nose like a cherry!

His droll little mouth was drawn

up like a bow.

And the beard of his chin was

as white as the snow;

Cat. 27 His eyes how they twinkled, 1902. Courtesy of William Wagner addressed his *Scarecrow and the Tin-Man* to "Little Freddie Stone," probably thinking that the star's first child, then on the way, would be a boy. (Instead it was a girl, Dorothy Stone, who later became a well-known actress.) The most effective advertising gimmick for *The Marvelous Land of Oz* was "Queer Visitors from the Marvelous Land of Oz" a Sunday comic page written by Baum and drawn by Walt MacDougall; Denslow replied with the short-lived "Denslow's Scarecrow and the Tin-Man" series that S. S. McClure syndicated from December 11, 1904, to March 12, 1905. While Baum went on to write a long successful series of Oz books, *Denslow's Scarecrow and The Tin-Man* soon went out of print.

In 1903 Ann Waters Denslow finally sued for divorce on the grounds of desertion. She had fallen in love with Lawrence Mazzanovich, a young landscape painter who was a friend of both Denslows. (He too had a studio in the Fine Arts Building; Denslow had taken him to East Aurora to work for the Roycrofters.) "Denslow was a pretty gruff old fellow," Hubbard's son

Page from *Denslow's Three Little Kittens,* 1904

Cat. 38 The Three Little Kittens, 1904

observed, "and I can well understand that a soft talking, nice guy like Mazzy didn't have too much trouble winning her away."[81] Ann Waters' action against the famous children's book illustrator made the Chicago papers. So did Denslow's rescue of a seventeen-year-old girl who had fallen in the Madison Square canal in New York City about the same time.[82] On Christmas Eve Denslow finally wed Frances Doolittle in New York City.

The couple then left for Bermuda to honeymoon in a kingdom all their own. "I have bought an island," Denslow informed Alfred Stieglitz, "just outside the harbor of Hamilton containing ten acres of rocks, soil, and cedar trees. On this island I am now building a mansion, a cottage and a dock. This keeps me busy in the afternoon while the books for babes takes up my time in the forenoon. As this is where I work to the best advantage I wish to make it as comfortable as possible."[83] Winters in Bermuda invigorated Denslow. He said he had never been so productive before. A book a year had been wearying for him, but once in Bermuda he effortlessly completed all the designs for the first twelve of "Denslow's Picture Books for Children."

On January 15, 1904, he declared himself

"King Denslow I" of the newly named Denslow Island. "Of course," he said, "in going ahead with the formation of my kingdom I have had to use the greatest diplomacy. If the government in Washington had got wind of it in the early stages, I have no doubt that they would have sent a fleet to Denslow Island to blow it out of the water. England, too, would have stepped in with a transport of troops, and the whole affair would have been off."[84] Then he appointed the captain of his yacht "Admiral of His Majesty's Navy," and his cook "Chief Steward and Keeper of the Accounts." "Now," Denslow explained, "I am fully equipped to meet all opposition. My navy, under the control of Captain and Admiral Archie, in splendid condition, with its full complement of men and guns, and while I have no army to speak of, I rely on the superior statesmanship of my cabinet to protect me from foreign foes." The rest of his "cabinet" consisted of his cook, who, "from the way he has handled the butcher and grocer," Denslow confidently predicted, "can successfully battle with any statesman the old or the new world may pit against him." Denslow completed his little kingdom by building a castle of the local sandstone, and from the balcony of its tall observatory tower he could look over the entire bay. From its turret flew a sea horse flag he designed.

In that "country of perpetual summer," Denslow followed a strict regimen of work and recreation. "Just as athletes go into training for a conquest,"

Cat. 31 Illustration for *Denslow's One Ring Circus,* 1903

he explained, "the busy man has to train and keep himself constantly fit for work. But if one enjoys the physical exercise the training is far from irksome; and when you know it is good for what ails you, you are apt to grow to like it even if you do not at first."[85] Up at dawn, he took his morning swim before breakfast; after eating, he went off to his studio to work until two o'clock. Then he sailed his yacht *Wizard* until sunset. Denslow's routine was much the same back in New York City in the warmer months. From his new Riverside Drive apartment, which had a grand view of the Hudson, his secretary looked after his correspondence and other business affairs and a Japanese servant cooked the meals and looked after the household. Done with work by early afternoon, Denslow went downtown for his daily exercise or to the Columbia Yacht Club. He also vacationed on Prince Edward Island, and the summer of 1904 he rented a house at Ponquogue, Long Island, near Good Ground on Shinnecock Bay, to work on his books. When not drawing, he went swimming, sailing, or fishing with his wife and little Frances. He also enjoyed golf, ice skating on the Hackensack River, and snowshoeing up in Canada in winter. Although an avid fisherman, Denslow had no interest in hunting and claimed he did not want his little readers to think that he might shoot any creature.

Part of every day was spent hard at the drawing board. "It was as good as a three-ring circus to see Den at work designing and making his draw-

ings," Charles Waldron reported. "He would have a different sketch tacked on to different boards, with his box of colors handy at his right hand. After working for an hour on one design until he was tired of the subject, he would then take a fresh drawing on another board." However simple his final pen-and-ink drawings appeared, a great deal of care went into each of them. Over and over he blocked out his characters in pencil and making frequent alterations until he got the exact gesture he wanted. Waldron noticed that "the figure might have as many as six different legs, four heads, and as many arms. When the right ones were selected, it would be drawn in with ink and the others erased. Meanwhile he smoked very mild tobacco in his corncob pipe, which was out at least half of the time, and would carry on an animated conversation and dictate business letters to his secretary."[86] He also smoked (appropriately) a sea horse brand of cigarette.

Another area in which Denslow was active was the theater. After *The Wizard of Oz* musical opened, producers sought him for other shows. The first was the new "musical fantasie" *The Land of Nod,* an obvious imitation of *The Wizard of Oz,* that opened at Chicago Opera House on June 12, 1905. For it Denslow designed the costumes for the Man in the Moon, April Fool, Welch Rarebit, Sandman, Telephone Man, and other odd characters. More important was *The Pearl and the Pumpkin,* a lavish musical extravaganza that Denslow both conceived and designed. He came up with a cast of eccentric characters and then thrashed out a plot. With preliminary sketches and a rough scenario under his arm, Denslow secured a meeting with A. L. Erlanger of Klaw and Erlanger, the country's most powerful theatrical syndicate. While discussing the action of the story and showing him the costume studies, Denslow promised Erlanger that the play, like his children's books, would contain only "pure wit and clean fun." There would be none of the standard Broadway gags in his musical. The producer was so impressed with the presentation that he agreed to back the show even without a finished libretto. He was obviously convinced that Denslow had the makings of a show that could well be another *Wizard of Oz,* and he did not hesitate to make it one of the most expensive productions of the time.

Having no experience as a playwright, Denslow sought help from Paul West, editor at the New York *World* who had commissioned the two "Father Goose" comic pages. West worked over Denslow's scenario with its vast cast of proverbial and historical figures (John Doe, Joe Miller, Davy Jones, Blackbeard, Captain Kidd, Ancient Mariner, Flying Dutchman, and Mother Carey's Chickens) to weave all these seemingly discordant elements into a passably comprehensible libretto. "Mr. West caught the spirit of the thing almost instantly," Denslow admitted. "I told him of my ideas, and showed him some of the sketches and the portion of the manuscript that he has already submitted is precisely what we want."[87] West proved to be a versatile (as well as volatile) lyricist, and working with composer John W. Bratton he came up with twenty-four numbers. "While, as you know, I have written every line of the book," West reminded Erlanger, "I am willing to share the responsibility with Mr. Denslow, who invented many of the characters and part of the original story."[88] But West also demanded that the lyrics be credited solely to himself.

In the meantime Denslow and West collaborated on a children's book based on the musical. *The Pearl and the Pumpkin* (1904) shamelessly imitated the format of *The Wonderful Wizard of Oz* with numerous colorplates and two-color textual illustrations, but West's story was far inferior to Baum's. As with the musical, locale and character were far more important than action. The hero is a boy named Joe Miller whose pumpkins everyone—from John Doe the baker to Ike Cannem the canner to the Ancient Mariner from Davy Jones' Locker—wants. Corn Dodger transforms Joe into a pumpkin-headed man (who bears a remarkable resemblance to Baum's Jack Pumpkinhead in *The Marvelous Land of Oz*), and Joe and his little friend Pearl Pringle go on a series of mild adventures on land and under the sea before the boy is finally restored to his right form.

Denslow's illustrations—125 pictures completed that summer on Long Island—were as good as

Denslow and his brother LeGrand Norton Denslow playing golf in England, ca. 1909.
Courtesy of the late Patricia Denslow Eykyn

ever. Particularly impressive were the different, distinctive characters set to appear in the forthcoming musical and the children's book. He was also clever in the introduction of comic fish throughout the tale. For the Davy Jones Crew, Denslow sought all that he could on the pirates of the Spanish Main, ransacking bookshops and auction houses in New York, Bermuda, and Barbados for out-of-print material, and going as far as London to purchase items from rare book dealer Bernard Quaritch. As a consequence of all this research, the characters of *The Pearl and the Pumpkin* lack the novelty of the Scarecrow, Tin Woodman, Cowardly Lion, and all the others in *The Wonderful Wizard of Oz*. Still it was a handsome children's book and evidently sold well.

Designing every aspect of the extravaganza while personally overseeing their execution on the stage taxed Denslow's inventiveness, time, and patience. The only book he had time to illustrate in 1905 was Richard Webb's minor satire *Me and Lawson* (1905) for which Denslow supplied a few caricatures. *The Pearl and the Pumpkin* required him to design multiple costumes changes for the more than 150 players as well as all the show's properties and lavish scenery. The locales shifted from a New England farm on Halloween to a canning factory in Bermuda, then on to the underwater world of Davy Jones's Locker, and finally to Mother Carey's

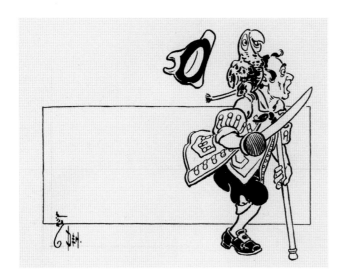

Cat. 39 Long John Silver, ca. 1904

fairy realm. To get the coloring and other details of the Bermuda scenes correct, Denslow dove thirty feet in Hamilton Harbour to study the vegetation, rocks, and wrecks; his helpers held water glasses over the water to prevent ripples while he painted in his dinghy near the coral reefs. Klaw and Erlanger made good their promise to mount a spectacular entertainment and made *The Pearl and the Pumpkin* one of the most expensive productions of the day. They even provided on stage an enormous mechanical whale containing a comfortably furnished apartment for Davy Jones. Because of its New England setting, they opened the handsome, tune-filled show in Boston on July 16, 1905; they followed it a month later with a respectful run on Broadway. The reviews were generally good, particularly for Denslow's sets and costumes, and the public evidently enjoyed the musical; however, Klaw and Erlanger's investment far exceeded the return. When the producers closed the show after only a year on the road, it was still in the red.

The financial disappointment could not have helped Denslow's reputation. He never lacked for novel ideas, but with a major failure like *The Pearl and the Pumpkin*, his career was quickly slipping out of his control. Over the years Denslow had created a school of illustration that inspired not only imitators but plagiarists as well, and probably all these copies ultimately hurt his career. Some of his pictures were pirated on postcards, sheet music, even a board game. In London, "Dean's David Brett Series" slavishly traded on "Denslow's Picture Books for Children." But the artist was finally spurred into action by McLoughlin Brothers' shameless imitation of *Denslow's 5 Little Pigs* in 1904; he and Dillingham brought a copyright infringement suit against the publisher and anyone who might sell it.[89] Denslow was also confronted by increased resistance to his new projects. He tried to revive interest in his old comic strip with *Billy Bounce* (1906), a children's book he co-wrote with Dudley A. Bragdon, a minor author of vaudeville sketches. This new fantasy was a poor imitation of *The Wizard of Oz,* and the pictures lacked Denslow's usual spark. Neither he nor Bragdon found a producer for "Billy Bounce and

Cat. 38 "Don't touch me," she cried, 1904

Boogieman," a musical extravaganza to be based on the book. They had better luck with a series of twelve "Ill Nature Studies," lightly satirical verses about parlor pests, which ran in the syndicated *Sunday Magazine* newspaper supplement (November 24, 1907-September 6, 1908).

One of Denslow's last children's books, Isabel M. Johnston's *Jeweled Toad* (1907), was based on another unproduced libretto. This minor children's story that made good use of various fairy traditions contained some of Denslow's prettiest illustrations, but it did not sell well. Denslow tried to return to the Sunday funnies in 1907, but none of the newspaper syndicates saw promise in the ambitious "Willie Wish and Zuni-aztec," just another imitation of Winsor McCay's "Little Nemo in Slumberland." Baum, Denslow, and Tietjens briefly put their differences aside to work on a proposed extravaganza based on *Father Goose,* but Klaw and Erlanger finally turned it down. Certainly the most promising of Denslow's many unrealized projects was a musical derived from Joel Chandler Harris' Uncle Remus stories with Br'er Rabbit and Br'er Fox as a Scarecrow and Tin Woodman comedy team. (Harris also wanted Denslow to illustrate a new collection of the tales.) Denslow, Tietjens, and Harris' son Julian LaRose Harris could not stop squabbling, and Klaw and Erlanger finally lost interest in the proposal.

As pressures from many unresolved projects were mounting, Denslow began drinking heavily again. Anticipating trouble, Frances tried to save what she could. About 1906 she finally left him and returned to Chicago to live with her sisters. When she filed for divorce in 1911, claiming desertion due to drunkenness, she stated that for the last six years Denslow's drinking had been "very nearly habitually, except at short intervals." "The conditions were unbearable," her daughter testified. Eunice Tietjens

Cat. 46 "*Denslow's Scarecrow and the Tin-Man with the Cowboys,*" 1904

supported their contentions, stating in court that Denslow "drank a great deal, caroused a great deal, is very unsettled, does not work," and "for the last five years he has seldom been sober."[90] Convinced that he could always get some employment, his wife sought alimony, but the court ruled that it lacked jurisdiction over him so long as he remained out of state. Denslow never bothered to defend himself, and the divorce was granted.

Despite his lack of sobriety during this period, Denslow indeed had been able to work, but he could no longer command the commissions or the fees he once did. He had been earning between a healthy $100 to $200 a week before his fortunes changed. The bulk of his income had actually come from the *Wizard of Oz* musical, but decreasing royalties from that show as it finally wound down its long prosperous run must have greatly strained his finances. Now he encountered more difficulty placing work, for at that time editors of children's books were far less tolerant of alcoholics than they are today.

In 1908 Denslow returned to advertising and moved to Buffalo to work for Niagara Lithograph Company. For this firm, he designed a remarkable series of pamphlets that capitalized on his reputation as "the leading juvenile illustrator in the world." These jolly giveaways for children promoted such varying products as Berry Brothers Varnishes (*Around the World in a Berry Wagon,* 1909), Duffy's Apple Juice (*Duffy's Apple Juice Imp*, 1909), Red Goose Shoes (*The Red Goose Book*, 1910), Force Malt Wheat Flake Breakfast Food (*Through Foreign Lands with "Sunny Jim,"* 1910), Johnston's Harvesters (*Johnnie Johnston's Airship*, 1910), Shinola Shoe Polish (*Everyday Heroes*, 1910), Minute Tapioca (*Boy Scouts,* 1911), and Fairbank's Fairy Soap (*Fairbank's Juvenile History of the United States,* 1911). And despite their ephemeral content, these brightly printed booklets were sometimes as delightfully decorated as the earlier "Denslow's Picture Books for Children". He also contributed to the postcard craze, designing a successful Thanksgiving Humor Series and advertising cards for Teddy Bear Bread and Chi-Namel Varnish.

One of the few publishers to welcome him was Elbert Hubbard; Denslow often traveled to East Aurora to supply his old friend with cartoons for the new Roycroft journal, the *Fra.* But Denslow's last major effort as a children's book illustrator was certainly a prestigious one: *When I Grow Up* was a series of poems he both wrote and illustrated for *St. Nicholas* (November 1908 to October 1909) and which the Century Company published as a picture book in 1909. Denslow accompanied his doggerel about what little boys want to be when they grow up with garish lithographs, many of them caricatures of such prominent Americans as Teddy Roosevelt (the soldier), William Jennings Bryan (the orator), William Gillette (the detective), Buffalo Bill Cody (the scout), and Denslow himself (the fisherman), in perhaps the most extensive use of color in the magazine's long history. But the good humor seems

Cat. 37 Denslow's Scarecrow and the Tin-man at the Flower Festival in California, 1904

Cat. 56 Willie Wish and Zuni-aztec, 1907

52

forced at times, and Denslow's line had lost its precision. *When I Grow Up* failed to revive his career.

Denslow long had been living far beyond his means. Perhaps he thought prosperity would reappear any minute. He went to England in 1909 to visit his brother, a trip he likely could ill afford. His Bermuda island was a luxury he could no longer justify, and he mortgaged the property to Tietjens in 1911. By 1913, he was back in New York City where he took engraver Alcan Moss as a partner and established The Denslow Company on Fifth Avenue. He wasted his last years working for Rosenbaum Studios, a second-rate art agency that made sheet music covers one of its specialties. Denslow even co-wrote with Moss the lyrics of a 1915 isolationist song, "Charity Begins at Home," with the following chorus:

> 'Tis just we help all Europe's poor,
> For they are stricken sore,
> But don't forget the needy ones
> We have before our door.
> I've traveled far, and in each land,
> Where e'er I've chanced to roam.
> I've always heard that Charity,
> Sweet gifts begin at home.
> Oh! Charity kind Charity,
> Help first our poor at home!

It was not good verse, but it did reflect his state of mind. Denslow could have used some charity himself. The agency paid him only a fraction of what he had once earned, and he was living in shabby bachelor quarters. On occasion he pawned or sold books and other belongings to get by. At his lowest he borrowed a dollar here, a dollar there from friends. Some of his better work at this time appeared in *John Martin's Book,* a new juvenile monthly, which, if like most children's magazines, probably did not pay well.

Denslow's luck seemed to be improving

Cat. 55 White Wings, the Fried Egg, ca. 1907.
Courtesy of the New York Public Library, Astor, Lenox, and Tilden Foundations

when he sold for a handsome fee a clever cover design to the humor magazine *Life* (July 15, 1915). His burlesque of the current fashion for Egyptian dress popularized by Paul Poiret and the Ballets Russes in Paris proved that Denslow still had the gift for caricature. But he threw the money away on a two-day binge, caught pneumonia, and died on March 29, 1915. He was 58 years old. None of the papers that had carried his pictures in the past bothered to publish an obituary of the once famous illustrator of *The Wonderful Wizard of Oz.* His will, made out on May 19, 1914, left his entire estate (which was valued at only $1,000) to Dorothy Federlein, a friend in Buffalo. He was quietly buried in Kensico Cemetery, Valhalla, New York.

Paul Tietjens once blamed his friend's failure in life on the success of *The Wizard of Oz* musical and concluded that "for Denslow's own good it certainly would have been better if he had not been given the means to drink himself to death."[91] Tietjens offered too easy a rationalization. Alcoholism is a disease, and perhaps a drunkard's worst enemy is intolerance. The musical's success may indeed have been the making and breaking of Denslow, but not in the way Tietjens suggested. Artists do not always know

Denslow at his drawing board, ca. 1910. Courtesy of the L. Frank Baum Papers, Syracuse University Library, Department of Special Collections.

where their true talents lie. Denslow squandered far too much of his time and ability trying to land another stage hit rather than concentrating on his children's books. Juvenile literature might have brought him a smaller immediate income, but in the end it could well have been a steadier one. Unfortunately for Denslow, too often those books he did choose to illustrate

were not of the first rank.

But the artistic quality of the pictures should not be judged merely on the literary merit of what they accompany. It is the style, the atmosphere, the invention, the overall spirit that an artist invokes through the drawings that finally lifts them above the commonplace. Denslow played a pivotal role in the history of American illustration. He produced some remarkable work in several branches of commercial art; his continuing influence can still be traced through children's books, comic strips, and even animated cartoons. Denslow's individualistic and easily recognizable manner of drawing made a profound contribution to twentieth century illustration.

Cover for *Life*, July 15, 1915. Courtesy of Michael Gessel

1 W. W. Denslow autograph book, August 13, 1901, courtesy C. Warren Hollister.

2 Eunice Tietjens, *The World at My Shoulder* (New York: Macmillan, 1938), p. 13.

3 Felix Shay, *Elbert Hubbard of East Aurora* (New York: William H. Wise, 1926), p. 149.

4 Denslow as quoted in Forrest Crissey, "William Wallace Denslow," *Carter's Monthly,* March 1898, pp. 269–70.

5 Denslow as quoted in Crissey, "Denslow," p. 270–71.

6 Denslow as quoted in "A Lover of Children Who Knows How to Make Them Laugh," Detroit *News,* September 13, 1903.

7 W. W. Denslow, "Poster Art," *Bill Poster,* September 1896, p. 14.

8 Denslow as quoted in New Orleans *Democrat,* November 11, 1899.

9 Charles W. Waldron, "Mother Goose in a New Gown," Lewiston, Maine, *Evening Journal Illustrated Magazine,* October 26, 1901.

10 Charles W. Lemon, "Deadheads De Luxe," n.d., courtesy Fred M. Meyer.

11 William W. Denslow vs. Annie Denslow, G. N. 177131 (January 18 and February 19, 1896), Superior Court Chancery, Cook County Records, Chicago.

12 Charles Lemon to Jack Snow, June 15, 1943, courtesy Fred M. Meyer. Fifty years later, Lemon was as bitter as ever towards Denslow; he insisted that *The Wonderful Wizard of Oz* was actually a story Denslow stole from another artist.

13 Denslow, "Poster Art," *Bill Poster,* January 1897, pp. 15–16.

14 Denslow as quoted in Crissey, "Denslow," p. 271.

15 "The Newspaper Artist at Work," San Francisco *Call,* January 1, 1893.

16 W. W. Denslow diary, March 26, 1893, courtesy C. Warren Hollister.

17 Denslow as quoted in Crissey, "Denslow," p. 173.

18 Denslow diary, March 16, 1893.

19 Denslow diary, July 17, 1893.

20 Denslow diary, May 16, 1893.

21 Denslow as quoted in Leroy Armstrong, "Up among the Clouds," Chicago *Herald,* May 21, 1893.

22 Denslow diary, May 3, 1893.

23 Denslow diary, May 10, 1893.

24 [Charles W. Waldron], "At Dinner with Denslow," Lewiston, Maine, *Saturday Journal Illustrated Magazine,* February 18, 1905.

25 Denslow to Florence Roberts, January 10, 1895, courtesy Wilson B. Roberts.

26 Denslow to Roberts, January 10, 1895.

27 Denslow, "Poster Art," *Bill Poster,* May 1897, p. 16.

28 Denslow to Alfred Stieglitz, February 22, 1903, Alfred Stieglitz Archives, Collection of American Literature, Beinecke Rare Book and Manuscript Library, Yale University.

29 Denslow as quoted in Elliott R. Carpenter, "The Seventh and Eighth Mugs," n.d., courtesy Herman Bieber.

30 Denslow, "Poster Art," *Bill Poster,* September 1896, p. 14.

31 Denslow, "Poster Art," *Bill Poster,* June 1897, p. 15.

32 Denslow, "Poster Art," *Bill Poster,* September 1896, p. 14.

33 Denslow to John N. Hilliard, January 14, 1896, private collection.

34 R. C. Campbell to Denslow, July 27, 1897, Exhibit "E," Denslow vs. American Advertising & Bill Posting Co., 196472-6736 (October 25, 1901), Circuit Court of Cook County Records, Chicago.

35 Denslow, "Poster Art," *Bill Poster,* April 1897, p. 16.

36 Denslow, "Poster Art," *Bill Poster,* June 1897, p. 15.

37 Denslow, "Poster Art," *Bill Poster,* March 1897, p. 16.

38 Denslow to Daniel E. Hudson, November 2, 1897, Daniel E. Hudson Papers, Notre Dame Archives, Notre Dame, Indiana.

39 Isadora Duncan, *My Life* (New York: Liveright, 1927), pp. 28-29.

40 "Alleges Error in Article," Chicago *Tribune,* September 28, 1903.

41 Leroy Armstrong, "W. W. Denslow, Illustrator," *Home Magazine,* October 1898, p. 329.

42 Charles Warren Stoddard to Daniel E. Hudson, June 15, 1898, Daniel E. Hudson Papers, Notre Dame Archives.

43 Denslow, "Poster Art," *Bill Poster,* April 1897, p. 16.

44 Denslow as quoted in Albert Lane, *Elbert Hubbard and His Works* (Worcester, Mass.: Blanchard Press, 1901), p. 82.

45 Elbert Hubbard as quoted in Charles F. Hamilton, *As Bees in Honey Drown* (South Brunswick and New York: Barnes, 1973), p. 158.

46 Denslow to Hubbard, July 20, 1896, as quoted in Justin G. Schiller, *L. Frank Baum and Related Oziana* (New York: Swann Galleries, 1978), no. 312.

47 Denslow as quoted in Lane, *Hubbard,* p. 83.

48 Elbert Hubbard II to Russell P. MacFall, August 11, 1958, L. Frank Baum Papers, George Arents Research Library, Syracuse University, Syracuse, New York.

49 Hubbard to MacFall, August 11, 1958.

50 Hubbard and Denslow as quoted in Lane, *Hubbard,* p. 86.

51 Lane, *Hubbard,* p. 82.

52 Denslow, "Poster Art," *Bill Poster,* September 1896, p. 15.

53 Ralph Fletcher Seymour, *Some Went This Way* (Chicago: privately printed, 1945), p. 46.

54 Harry Neal Baum, "How Father Wrote the Oz Books," *American Book Collector,* December 1962, p. 17.

55 Hubbard as quoted in Chicago *Dispatch,* December 16, 1899.

56 Twain as quoted in Chicago *Tribune,* December 18, 1899.

57 Paul West to W. W. Denslow, December 6, 1899, L. Frank Baum Papers.

58 When Baum wrote *Father Goose's Year Book* (1907) he had Walter J. Enright do the pictures.

59 Undated letter of agreement between Baum and Denslow, early 1899, Baum Trust Papers, Woodland Hills, California.

60 Denslow as quoted in Harrison Decker, "An Artist Outdoors," *Outdoors,* September 1904, p. 276-77.

61 Denslow as quoted in "Denslow: Denver Artist, Originator of Scarecrow and Tin Man," Denver *Republican,* September 4, 1904.

62 Denslow as quoted in Waldron, "Mother Goose in a New Dress."

63 From a printer's proof of the artist's statement, private collection.

64 Denslow as quoted in "Denslow: Denver Artist."

65 Frederic W. Goudy, *A Half-Century of Type Design and Typography,* 1895-1946 (New York: Typophiles, 1946) pp. 48–50, 55.

66 George Ade as quoted in *Bookseller,* November 1901, p. 517.

67 Caroline M. Hewins, "Book Reviews, Book Lists, and Articles on Children's Reading," *Library Journal,* August 1901, p. 59.

68 Anne Carroll Moore, *A List of Books Recommended for a Children's Library,* prepared for Iowa Library Commission, circa 1902.

69 Denslow as quoted in "Lover of Children."

70 Denslow as quoted in "Denslow: Denver Artist."

71 Denslow and Baum did join forces to get back the plates for their books from George W. Ogilvie, who took over George M. Hill Co. when it went bankrupt in 1902. Ogilvie stapled together some old sheets of the colorplates of *The Wonderful Wizard of Oz,* printed a new story by Thomas H. Russell on the versos, slapped a new cover on the pamphlet, and called it *Pictures from The Wonderful Wizard of Oz* (1902). Only Denslow's name appeared on the title page. When Baum and Denslow secured the printing plates and Bobbs-Merrill reissued *The Wonderful Wizard of Oz* as *The New Wizard of Oz* in 1903, Denslow provided the new cover, endpaper, and title-page designs.

72 Baum-Denslow-Tietjens contract, September 21, 1901, Baum Trust Papers.

73 Paul Tietjens to Julian LaRose Harris, May 14, 1905, Harris Papers, Emory University, Atlanta, Georgia.

74 Certificate of Evidence (September 16, 1903), Ann Holden Denslow vs. W. W. Denslow, G. N. 232,135, Cook County Records, Chicago.

75 Denslow diary, May 12, 1893.

76 Denslow, "Poster Art," *Bill Poster,* February 1897, p. 14.

77 Six of the best of the 18 picture books (*5 Little Pigs; Old Mother Hubbard; Simple Simon; House That Jack Built; Mary Had a Little Lamb; Animal Fair*) were collected as *Denslow's Picture Book Treasury* (New York: Arcade Publishing, 1990).

Cat. 67 Print, "What's the Use?," 1899.
Courtesy of the Newberry Library, Chicago

78 Denslow as quoted in "Lover of Children."

79 Denslow as quoted in "Denslow: Denver Artist."

80 Denslow as quoted in G. W. Dillingham press release for Denslow's Picture Books, 1903, private collection.

81 Hubbard to MacFall, August 11, 1958.

82 See "Artist Denslow Rescues a Drowning Girl," Chicago *Tribune,* August 14, 1903.

83 Denslow to Stieglitz, February 23, 1904, Alfred Stieglitz Archives. The island (formerly known as Harris or Dyer Island, now Buck's Island) is actually 4 acres, not 10.

84 Denslow as quoted in "Denver Artist Rules an Island," Denver *Republican,* January 17, 1904.

85 Denslow as quoted in Decker, "Artist Outdoors," p. 277.

86 Waldron, "A Peep into Bohemia," Lewiston, Maine, *Saturday Journal Illustrated Magazine,* February 21–26, 1903.

87 Denslow as quoted in "Denslow: Denver Artist."

88 Paul West to A. L. Erlanger, January 6, 1905, Schubert Archive, New York City.

89 "M'Loughlin Brothers' 'Five Little Pigs' Enjoined," *Publishers Weekly,* January 16, 1904, p. 67; G. W. Dillingham Co. to Librarian of Congress, April 14, 1904, Copyright Office, Washington, D.C.

90 Frances Denslow vs. William W. Denslow, G. N. 306,402 (July 19, 1911), Circuit Court of Cook County Records, Chicago.

91 Paul Tietjens to Maud Gage Baum, May 20, 1940, Baum Trust Papers.

"An American King on a Bermuda Island,"
Philadelphia *North American,* February 28, 1904.

Bader, Barbara. *American Picturebooks from Noah's Ark to the Beast Within.* New York: Macmillan, 1976.

Bowles, J. M. "Children's Books for Children," *Brush and Pencil,* September 1903.

Gangloff, Deborah. *The Artist, the Book, and the Child.* Lockport: Illinois State Museum, Lockport Gallery, 1989.

Greene, Douglas G. "W. W. Denslow: A Checklist," *Baum Bugle,* Autumn 1992.

————, and Michael Patrick Hearn. *W. W. Denslow.* Mount Pleasant, Michigan: Central Michigan University, Clarke Historical Library, 1976.

Hearn, Michael Patrick. "An American Illustrator and His Posters," *American Book Collector,* May-June 1982.

————. *The Annotated Wizard of Oz.* New York: Clarkson N. Potter, 1976.

————. "W. W. Denslow, the Forgotten Illustrator," *American Artist,* May 1973.

Norcia, Ernest. "An Artist's Appreciation of W. W. Denslow," *Baum Bugle,* Autumn 1992.

"Special Number [W. W. Denslow]," *American Book Collector,* December 1964.

Thompson, Susan Otis. *American Book Design and William Morris.* New York: R. E. Bowker, 1977.

Cat. 78 Bookplate for Charles M. Wilkins, ca. 1900.
Courtesy of the Chapin Library, Williams College

1) *Elbert Hubbard and others associated with the Roycroft Press,* March 1898
Pencil on paper, 10 3/4 × 8 3/8" (27.3 × 21.3cm)
Private collection

2) *Captain Bing Was a Pirate King*, 1899
Ink and watercolor on paper,
Sight size 19 × 16" (48.3 × 40.6 cm)
Illustration for L. Frank Baum. *Father Goose, His Book* (Chicago: Geo. M. Hill Co., 1899) [p. 37]
The Betsy B. Shirley American Children's Literature Collection, Beinecke Library, Yale University

3) *The Clock-Work Man,* ca. 1899
Pencil on paper, 10 7/8 × 8 3/8" (27.6 × 21.3 cm)
Study for L. Frank Baum. *Father Goose, His Book.* (Chicago: Geo. M. Hill Co., 1899)
Private Collection

4) *The Clock-Work Man,* ca. 1899
Ink over pencil on paper,
23 1/2 × 11" (59.7 × 27.9 cm)
Two illustrations for L. Frank Baum. *Father Goose, His Book.* (Chicago: Geo. M. Hill Co., 1899), [p.15]
Private Collection

5) *Father Goose, His Book,* 1899
Ink over pencil on paper,
13 3/8 × 10 1/4" (34.0 × 26.0 cm)
Cover illustration for L. Frank Baum. *Father Goose, His Book.* (Chicago: Geo. M. Hill Co., 1899)
Print Collection, The Miriam and Ira D. Wallach Division of Art, The New York Public Library, Astor, Lenox and Tilden Foundations

6) *Father Goose, His Book,* 1899
Ink on paper, sight size 10 7/8 × 18 7/8"
Dust jacket design for L. Frank Baum. *Father Goose, His Book.* (Chicago: Geo. M. Hill Co., 1899)

The Betsy B. Shirley American Children's Literature Collection, Beinecke Library, Yale University

7) *Mother Goose Became Quite New,* ca. 1899
Pencil on paper, 10 7/8 × 8 3/8" (27.6 × 21.3 cm)
Study for L. Frank Baum. *Father Goose, His Book.* (Chicago: Geo. M. Hill Co., 1899)
Private collection

8) *Untitled,* 1899
Ink on paper,
sight size 23 1/8 × 18 1/2" (59.1 × 47.0 cm)
Illustration for L. Frank Baum.
Father Goose, His Book. (Chicago: Geo. M. Hill Co., 1899), [p.45]
The Edith and Warren Hollister Oz Collection

9) *Old Bill Spear, Quincy, Mass.* 1899
Ink on paper, sight size 13 × 10" (33.0 × 25.4 cm)
Illustration for *The Philistine,* October 1899
Private Collection

10) *Chapter V. The Rescue of the Tin Woodman,* 1900
Ink on paper, 15 × 9 1/8" (38.1 × 23.2 cm)
Illustration for L. Frank Baum. *The Wonderful Wizard of Oz.* (Chicago and New York: Geo. M. Hill Co., 1900), [p.51].
Print Collection, The Miriam and Ira D. Wallach Division of Art, The New York Public Library, Astor, Lenox and Tilden Foundations

11) *Chapter VI. The Cowardly Lion,* 1900
Ink on paper, 11 3/8 × 10 7/8" (28.9 × 27.6 cm)
Illustration for L. Frank Baum. *The Wonderful Wizard of Oz.* (Chicago and New York: Geo. M. Hill Co., 1900), [p.63].
Print Collection, The Miriam and Ira D. Wallach Division of Art, The New York Public Library, Astor, Lenox and Tilden Foundations

12) *Chapter VIII. The Deadly Poppy Field,* 1900
Ink on paper, 15 1/4 × 12 (38.7 × 30.5 cm)
Illustration for L. Frank Baum. *The Wonderful Wizard of Oz.*(Chicago and New York: Geo. M. Hill Co., 1900),[p.85].
Print Collection, The Miriam and Ira D. Wallach Division of Art, The New York Public Library, Astor, Lenox and Tilden Foundations

13) *Chapter XI. The Wonderful Emerald City of Oz,* 1900
Ink on paper, 14 1/2 × 11 1/4" (36.8 × 28.6 cm)
Illustration for L. Frank Baum's *The Wonderful Wizard of Oz.* (Chicago and New York: Geo. M. Hill Co., 1900), [p. 119].
Print Collection, The Miriam and Ira D. Wallach Division of Art, The New York Public Library, Astor, Lenox and Tilden Foundations

14) *Exactly So! I am a Humbug,* 1900
Ink on paper, 9 1/4 × 11 1/2" (23.5 × 29.2 cm)
Illustration for L. Frank Baum. *The Wonderful Wizard of Oz* (Chicago and New York: Geo. M. Hill Co., 1900), [p. 185].
Print Collection, The Miriam and Ira D. Wallach Division of Art, The New York Public Library, Astor, Lenox and Tilden Foundations

15) *The Tin Woodman and the Scarecrow,* 1900
Ink on paper, sight size 16 1/2 × 17" (41.9 × 43.2 cm)
Illustration for L. Frank Baum. *The Wonderful Wizard of Oz* (Chicago and New York: Geo. M. Hill Co., 1900), p. 71.
The Betsy B. Shirley American Children's Literature Collection, Beinecke Library, Yale University

16) *Untitled,* 1900
Ink on paper,
Sight size 20 3/4 × 14 1/4" (52.7 × 36.2 cm)
Copyright page for L. Frank Baum. *The Wonderful Wizard of Oz* (Chicago and New York: Geo. M. Hill Co., 1900)
The Edith and Warren Hollister Oz Collection

17) *Untitled,* 1900
Ink over pencil,
Sight size 20 1/4 × 14 1/4" (51.4 × 36.2 cm)
Endpaper design for L. Frank Baum. *The Wonderful Wizard of Oz* (Chicago and New York: Geo. M. Hill Co., 1900)
The Edith and Warren Hollister Oz Collection

18) *Untitled,* 1900
Ink over pencil on paper,
Sight size 14 5/8 × 10 1/2 " (37.2 × 26.7 cm)
Titlepage for L. Frank Baum. *The Wonderful Wizard of Oz* (Chicago and New York: Geo. M. Hill Co., 1900)
The Edith and Warren Hollister Oz Collection

19) *The Wonderful Wizard of Oz,* ca. 1900
Watercolor over pencil on paper,
Sight size 8 5/8 × 14 3/8" (21.9 × 36.5 cm)
Cover design for L. Frank Baum. *The Wonderful Wizard of Oz* (Chicago and New York: Geo. M. Hill Co., 1900)
The Edith and Warren Hollister Oz Collection

20) *You Ought to be Ashamed of Yourself!* 1900
Ink on paper, 15 1/4 × 11 1/2" (38.7 × 29.2 cm)
Illustration for L. Frank Baum. *The Wonderful Wizard of Oz.* (Chicago and New York: Geo. M. Hill Co., 1900), p. 67.
Print Collection, The Miriam and Ira D. Wallach Division of Art, The New York Public Library, Astor, Lenox and Tilden Foundations

21) *The Songs of Father Goose,* 1900
Ink on paper, sight size 15 × 11 3/4 " (38.1 × 28.6 cm)
Cover illustration for L. Frank Baum. *The Songs of Father Goose for the Kindergarten, the Nursery and the Home* (Chicago and New York: George M. Hill Company, 1900)
The Betsy B. Shirley American Children's Literature Collection, Beinecke Library, Yale University

22) *Denslow's Mother Goose,* 1901
Ink and gouache on blue paper,
12 × 9" (30.5 × 22.9 cm)
Color sketch for W.W. Denslow. *Denslow's Mother Goose* (New York: McClure, Phillips & Company Publishers, 1901)
Print Collection, The Miriam and Ira D. Wallach Division of Art, The New York Public Library, Astor, Lenox and Tilden Foundations

23) *Untitled,* 1901
Ink over pencil,
Sight size 21 × 20 1/8" (53.3 × 51.1 cm)
Endpaper design for W.W. Denslow. *Denslow's Mother Goose* (New York: McClure, Phillips & Company, 1901)
The Betsy B. Shirley American Children's Literature Collection, Beinecke Library, Yale University

24) *John de Luxe* [caricature of Elbert Hubbard], 1900
Ink on paper, 10 1/2 × 6 1/4" (26.7 × 16.5 cm)
Print Collection, The Miriam and Ira D. Wallach Division of Art, The New York Public Library, Astor, Lenox and Tilden Foundations

25) *Denslow's Night Before Christmas,* 1902
Ink on paper, 14 3/4 × 11 1/2" (37.5 × 29.2 cm)
Titlepage for *Denslow's Night Before Christmas.* New York: G. W. Dillingham Co., 1902
Collection of Beth and George Meredith

26) *Four designs for a nursery frieze,* ca. 1910-1920
Watercolor and ink on paper,
each approx. 3 3/8 × 7 1/4" (8.6 × 18.4 cm)
The Edith and Warren Hollister Oz Collection

27) *His Eyes How They Twinkled,* 1902
Ink on paper, each 15 1/8 × 11" (38.4 × 28 cm)
Double-page illustration for *Denslow's Night Before Christmas* (New York: G.W. Dillingham Co., 1902), [pp.46-47].
Collection of Beth and George Meredith

28) *Untitled,* 1902
Ink on paper, 14 1/2 × 22 1/2" (36.8 × 57.2 cm)
Endpaper design for *Denslow's Night Before Christmas* (New York: G.W. Dillingham Co., 1902)
Collection of Beth and George Meredith

29) *Denslow's House That Jack Built,* 1903
Ink over pencil on paper,
Sight size 16 3/8 × 11 7/8" 41.6 × 30.2 cm)
Cover illustration for *Denslow's House That Jack Built.* (New York: G. W. Dillingham, 1903)
The Edith and Warren Hollister Oz Collection

30) *Denslow's Little Red Riding Hood,* 1903
Ink over pencil on paper,
16 × 12 7/8" (40.6 × 32.7 cm)
Cover illustration for *Denslow's Little Red Riding Hood* (New York: G.W. Dillingham, 1903)
Private Collection

31) *Denslow's One Ring Circus,* 1903
Ink over pencil on paper,
15 3/8 × 12" (39.1 × 30.5 cm)
Illustration for *Denslow's One Ring Circus and Other Stories*
(New York: G.W. Dillingham, 1903) p. 6
Private Collection

32) *Denslow's Zoo,* 1903
Ink over pencil
Cover illustration for *Denslow's Zoo* (New York: G.W. Dillingham Co., 1903)
Kerlan Collection, University of Minnesota

33) *The Giant,* 1903
Ink on illustration board,
14 1/2 × 10 3/8" (36.9 × 26.4 cm)
Illustration for *Jack and the Bean-stalk* (New York:
G.W. Dillingham, Co., 1903), [p. 7].
Collection of the Brandywine River Museum, Gift
of Jane Collette Wilcox

34) *Untitled,* 1903
Ink over pencil on paper adhered to illustration
board, 11 × 8 1/2" (27.9 × 21.6 cm)
Illustration for *Denslow's Little Red Riding Hood*
(New York: G.W. Dillingham, 1903), [p.7].
The de Grummond Children's Literature Research
Collection, University of Southern Mississippi

35) *Untitled,* 1903
Ink over pencil on paper,
Sight size 14 1/2 × 10" (36.8 × 25.4 cm)
Illustration for *Denslow's Mary Had a Little Lamb*
(New York: G. W. Dillingham, 1903), [p. 11].
The Edith and Warren Hollister Oz Collection

36) *Chapter X. The Magic Spring,* 1904
Ink over pencil on paper, 13 3/8 × 9 5/8"
Pictorial chapter heading for W. W. Denslow and
Paul West. *The Pearl and the Pumpkin* (New York:
G.W. Dillingham, 1904), p. 102
Private Collection

37) *Denslow's Scarecrow and the Tin-Man at the
Flower Festival in California,* 1904
Ink over pencil on illustration board,
25 3/8 × 20 3/4" (63.9 × 52.7 cm)
Illustration for newspaper comic page
Private Collection

38) *"Don't touch me," she cried,* 1904
Ink over pencil on paper,
13 1/2 × 10" (34.3 × 25.4 cm)
Full-page illustration for W.W. Denslow and Paul
West. *The Pearl and the Pumpkin* (New York:
G.W. Dillingham, 1904), opp. p. 82
Private Collection

39) *Long John Silver,* ca. 1904
Ink on paper, 8 × 10" (20.3 × 25.4 cm)
Illustration for Paul West and W.W. Denslow.
The Pearl and the Pumpkin (New York: G.W.
Dillingham Co., 1904), p. 215
Collection of the Brandywine River Museum

40) *The Three Little Kittens,* 1904
Ink over pencil on paper,
20 × 13 3/8" (50.8 × 34.0 cm)
Illustration for *Denslow's Three Little Kittens*
(New York: G.W. Dillingham, 1904), p. 4
Private Collection

41) *Untitled,* ca. 1905
Ink on paper, 6 3/8 × 11 7/8" (16.2 × 30.2 cm)
Iillustration for "Denslow's Scarecrow and Tin-Man
Captured by Indians," February 26, 1905
Collection of Fred M. Meyer

42) *Untitled,* ca. 1905
Ink on paper, 6 1/2 × 8 5/8" (16.5 × 21.9 cm)
Iillustration for "Denslow's Scarecrow and Tin-Man
Captured by Indians," February 26, 1905
Collection of Fred M. Meyer

43) *Untitled,* ca. 1905
Ink on paper, 7 1/8 × 7 7/8" (18.1 × 20.0)
Iillustration for "Denslow's Scarecrow and Tin-Man
at the Carnival in New Orleans," February 19, 1905
Collection of Fred M. Meyer

44) *Untitled,* ca. 1905
Ink on paper, 6 1/2 × 4 3/4" (16.5 × 12.1 cm)
Illustration for "Denslow's Scarecrow and Tin-Man
on the Water," January 15, 1905
Collection of Fred M. Meyer

45) *Untitled,* ca. 1905
Ink on paper, 8 7/8 × 6 1/2" (22.6 × 16.5 cm)
Illustration for "Denslow's Scarecrow and Tin-Man
on the Water," January 15, 1905
Collection of Fred M. Meyer

46) *Untitled,* ca. 1905
Ink on paper, 6 3/8 × 9 5/8" (16.2 × 24.5 cm)
Illustration for "Denslow's Scarecrow and Tin-Man
with the Cowboys," March 5, 1905
Collection of Fred M. Meyer

47) *Untitled,* ca. 1905
Ink on paper, 7 1/2 × 14" (19.1 × 35.6 cm)
Illustration for "Denslow's Scarecrow and Tin-Man
in Yucatan," February 12, 1905
Collection of Fred M. Meyer

48) *Untitled,* ca. 1905
Ink on paper, 8 1/2 × 11 7/8" (22.6 × 30.3 cm)
Illustration for "Denslow's Scarecrow and Tin-Man
Shipwrecked," February 5, 1905
Collection of Fred M. Meyer

49) *Ancient Mariner,* ca. 1905
Pencil on paper, 9 7/8 × 7 7/8" (22.6 × 20.0 cm)
Costume study for the musical extravaganza,
The Pearl and the Pumpkin, by Paul West and
W. W. Denslow, 1905
Private Collection

50) *Ancient Mariner,* ca. 1905
Watercolor over pencil on paper,
10 × 7 7/8" (25.4 × 20.0 cm)
Costume study the musical extravaganza, *The Pearl
and the Pumpkin,* by Paul West and W. W.
Denslow, 1905
Private Collection

51) *Captain Jinks,* ca. 1905
Ink over pencil on paper, 10 × 8" (25.4 × 20.3 cm)
Costume study the musical extravaganza, *The Pearl
and the Pumpkin,* by Paul West and W. W.
Denslow, 1905
Private Collection

52) *Davey Jones' Locker,* ca. 1905
Watercolor over pencil on illustration board,
10 × 14" ((25.4 × 35.6 cm)
Stage design for the musical extravaganza of
The Pearl and the Pumpkin, by Paul West and
W. W. Denslow, 1905
Private Collection

53) *Miss Remington,* ca. 1905
Ink over pencil on paper,
10 1/4 × 8 1/4" (26/0 × 21/0 cm)
Costume study for the musical extravaganza,
The Pearl and the Pumpkin, by Paul West and
W. W. Denslow, 1905
Private Collection

54) *Mother Carey's Chickens,* ca. 1905
Watercolor over pencil on paper,
10 × 8 (25.4 × 20.3 cm)
Costume study for the musical extravaganza of
The Pearl and the Pumpkin, by Paul West and
W. W. Denslow, 1905
Private Collection

55) *White Wings, the Fried Egg,* 1907
Watercolor over pencil on paper,
15 1/4 × 11" (38.7 × 27.9 cm)
Costume study for the unproduced Broadway musi-
cal "Billy Bounce and Boogieman" by
W. W. Denslow and Dudley A. Bragdon.
Print Collection, The Miriam and Ira D. Wallach
Division of Art, The New York Public Library, Astor,
Lenox and Tilden Foundations

56) *Willie Wish and Zuni-Aztec,* 1907
Watercolor and ink over pencil on paper,
sight 26 1/4 × 20 3/8" (66.7 × 50.8 cm)
Illustration for an unpublished comic page
Private Collection

Posters and Prints

57) *Easton, Pennsylvania, in 1876 viewed from
Mt. Parnassus, Phillipsburg, N.J.,* 1876
Lithograph, 13 7/8 × 22 1/2" (35.3 × 57.2 cm)
Designed by W.W. Denslow, published by Peter
Fritz, successor to Reading Publishing House
Collection of the Palmer Museum of Art,
The Pennsylvania State University

58) *Chambersburg, Pennsylvania,* 1877
Lithograph, 16 1/4 × 22" (41.2 × 55.9 cm)
Designed by W.W. Denslow, Published by Peter
Fritz, successor to Reading Publishing House
Collection of the Palmer Museum of Art,
The Pennsylvania State University

59) *Merchant Prince of Cornville,* 1895
Letterpress, 21 × 12 3/4" (53.3 × 32.4 cm)
Book poster for Rand, McNally & Company,
Chicago
Private Collection

60) *Uncle Sam,* 1895
Letterpress, 14 1/8 × 10 5/8" (35.9 × 27.0 cm)
Poster for *Uncle Sam*
Private Collection

61) *Imitation of a Newsboy Selling the Herald to a
Haughti Lady,* 1896
Letterpress, 22 1/4 × 16 3/8" (56.5 × 41.6 cm)
Poster for the Chicago *Herald*
Private Collection

62) *Rosemary and Rue,* 1896
Letterpress, 24 7/8 × 17 1/2" (63.2 × 44.5 cm)
Book poster for Rand, McNally & Company,
Chicago
Private Collection

63) *Why Travel?,* ca. 1896
Letterpress,
sight size 13 1/4 × 17 1/8" (33.7 × 43.5 cm)
Book poster for *Rand, McNally Standard Atlas of
the World.* (H. B. Claflin, Co., ca. 1896)
Collection of Bert and Ellen Denker

64) *In the Shadow of the Pyramids,* 1897
Letterpress, 15 3/4 × 11 3/4" (40.0 × 29.8 cm)
Book poster
Private Collection

65) *The Marbeau Cousins,* 1898
Letterpress, 16 × 11" (40.6 × 27.9 cm)
Book poster
Private Collection

66) *Father Goose, His Book,* 1899
Letterpress, 14 1/2 × 11 1/8" (36.8 × 28.3 cm)
Book poster
Private Collection

67) *What's the Use?* by W. W. Denslow, 1899
Photograveur, 11 × 7 3/4" (27.9 × 19.7 cm)
Reproduction print, Roycroft Press, East Aurora, N.Y.
Collection of the Newberry Library, Chicago

68) *The Wonderful Wizard of Oz,* 1900
Letterpress,
Sight size 10 1/4 × 14 5/8" (26.0 × 37.2 cm)
Book poster for George M. Hill Co., Chicago and
New York
The Betsy B. Shirley American Children's Literature
Collection, Beinecke Library, Yale University

69) *Denslow's Night Before Christmas,* 1902
Letterpress, 12 × 18 1/4" (30.5 × 46.4 cm)
Book poster for G. W. Dillingham, Co., New York
Private Collection

70) *Hand-colored proof for endpapers,* 1902
Photoengraving on paper,
13 1/4 × 20" (33.1 × 50.8 cm)
Reproduction proofs for *Denslow's Night Before
Christmas,* G.W. Dillingham Co., New York
Collection of Beth and George Meredith

71) *Nursery frieze,* ca. 1910-1920
Lithograph on paper,
sight size 10 1/4 × 26 7/8" (26.0 × 68.3 cm)
Publisher unknown
Captioned: "The Tin Man must in a shower of rain
got rust in every joint, so he must carry an oil can
his elbows to annoint. Next came a lion cowardly
as timid as a bird, yet if some danger threatened
Dot his might roar was heard."
Private Collection

72) *Nursery frieze,* ca. 1910-1920
Lithograph on paper,
sight size 10 1/4 × 26 7/8" (26.0 × 68.3 cm)
Publisher unknown
Captioned: "The wicked witch the motor man and
Trixy sweet as honey, Gabriel the poet boy all thought
the Scarecrow funny. For he and Dot and Tin Man
too danced all a merry measure. To please the people
one and all and give the Wizard pleasure."
Private Collection

Selected Books and other Items

73) Vernon Lee [pseud. of Violet Paget], *Art and Life*
(East Aurora, N.Y.: Roycrofters, 1896) Hand-colored
initial designs and illustrations by W. W. Denslow
Private Collection

74) Samuel Taylor Coleridge. *So This Then is Ye Rime of
Ye Ancient Mariner.* East Aurora, N. Y.: Roycroft, 1899
Initial designs, front cover, and head- and tail-piece
designs by W.W. Denslow.
Collection of the Chapin Library of Rare Books,
Williams College, Williamstown, Massachusetts,
Gift of Geraldine Droppers Pomeroy

75) *The Sonnets of Shakespeare* (East Aurora, N.Y.:
Roycroft, 1899
Initial designs by W. W. Denslow
Collection of the Chapin Library of Rare Books,
Williams College, Williamstown, Massachusetts,
Gift of Geraldine Droppers Pomeroy

76) R.D. Blackmore *Lorna Doone* (Chicago: Rand,
McNally Company, 1897)
Collection of the Chapin Library of Rare Books,
Williams College, Williamstown, Massachusetts,
Gift of Robert L. Volz

77) Roycroft andirons with seahorse motif ca. 1896
Designed by W. W. Denslow
Wrought iron,
19 3/4 × 13 × 23 3/8" (50.2 × 33.0 × 59.34 cm)
Collection of Mrs. Andrew Wyeth

78) Bookplate of Charles M. Wilkins, designed by W. W.
Denslow, ca. 1900
3 3/4 × 2 3/4" (9.5 × 7.0 cm)
Collection of the Chapin Library of Rare Books,
Williams College, Williamstown, Massachusetts,
Gift of Ruth M. Sabin

79) Bookplate of Edna Browning Wilkins, designed by
W. W. Denslow, ca. 1901
5 × 3 1/2" (12.7 × 8.9 cm)
The Betsy B. Shirley American Children's Literature
Collection, Beinecke Library, Yale University

80) Copper-plate for bookplate of Edna Browning
Wilkins, ca. 1901
The Betsy B. Shirley American Children's Literature
Collection, Beinecke Library, Yale University

81) Ceramic plate with design of the "Queen of
Hearts," from *Denslow's Mother Goose,* ca. 1901
Manufactured by Haynes, Baltimore
Private Collection

82) W. W. Denslow. *When I Grow Up.* (New York:
Century Company, 1909)
The Betsy B. Shirley American Children's Literature
Collection, Beinecke Library, Yale University

Cover for
*Denslow's New
Series of Picture
Books for
Children,* 1904.
Courtesy of
Columbia
University Library.

64